THE ABODE
OF THE BELOVED

Rajinder Singh

PRAISE FOR SANT RAJINDER SINGH'S BOOKS

"This outstanding handbook reflects Sant Rajinder Singh's deep wisdom and realizations emerging from divine love and inner fulfillment."
– Deepak Chopra

"A powerful, deep, clearly written book about practical spirituality that helps us let go of the self-made blocks that interfere with the awareness that we are one with God and each other, that there is no separation, and that our soul is present and fully alive forever."
– Gerald G. Jampolsky, M.D.,
Author of *Love Is Letting Go of Fear*

"Firmly rooted in traditional wisdom, the author faces contemporary questions and challenges squarely and in a non-sectarian way...to bring the seed of peace within us to fruition in daily life and the world we live in."
– Brother David-Steindl Rast

"Sant Rajinder Singh's new book is food for the soul. It is an inspiring and informative source that speaks to both beginners and experienced travelers on the path of life. I was uplifted as I read this book, and re-dedicate myself to honoring my inner work."
– Steven Halpern,
Educator, Recording Artist, and Musician

"*Meditation empowers us in two spiritual arenas. First, it leads us to inner peace and fulfillment....Second, meditation allows us to use our talents and skills to make the world a better place to live. Sant Rajinder Singh elaborates on these ideas beautifully. He says that by mastering meditation, we not only attain personal fulfillment, we become an instrument for bringing peace and joy to those around us.*"

– Mary Nurrie Stearns,
Editor, *Personal Transformation*

"*...Sant Rajinder Singh expounds his theory that true peace and happiness can only come from within: the skill lies in learning how to tap into them.*"

– *Here's Health* magazine

THE ABODE OF THE

Beloved

Rajinder Singh

SK Publications

4 S 175 Naperville Rd., Naperville, IL 60563

www.sos.org

Publishing History

This edition first published by SK Publications 2015

1   3   5   7   9   11   13   15   14   12   10   8   6   4   2

© Copyright 2015 SK Publications

Naperville, Illinois, U.S.A.

ISBN 978-0-918224-78-1

Library of Congress Control Number: 2012944555

Printed in India by SK Publications, India

at Replika Press Pvt. Ltd.

TABLE OF CONTENTS

INTRODUCTION

When we awaken spiritually, a burning question arises as to how we can attain God-realization in our lifetime. We wonder how to accelerate our progress to meet that goal as quickly as possible.

As people gathered from all over the world for a spiritual holiday program, there seemed no better way to celebrate that time than to focus on ways to increase our spiritual development. The beautiful verses of the poet-saint, Sant Darshan Singh Ji Maharaj (1921-1989) touch on and illumine many aspects of spirituality. Through exploring the deeper meaning of his verses, we can gain insight and inspiration to speed our progress on the spiritual path.

These inspiring verses in this book focus on what we can gain by coming to the Abode of the Beloved, a spiritual Master. His teachings, inspiration, and the divine radiation of his presence uplift our soul to our ultimate goal of union with the Divine. May this book serve as a blueprint for those on the spiritual way to speed their reunion with God. Along with daily, regular meditation on the inner Light and Sound of God, ethical living, attending satsang, and selfless service performed with a heart full of love for God and one's fellow beings, the upliftment received at the abode of the Beloved can further accelerate one's spiritual journey. The grace of the spiritual Master stirs within us a ruling passion and zeal to tread the pathway back to God. The culmination of this inner journey is divine love, eternal bliss, and lasting happiness.

May this collection of talks fill every heart with light, love, and joy.

– RAJINDER SINGH

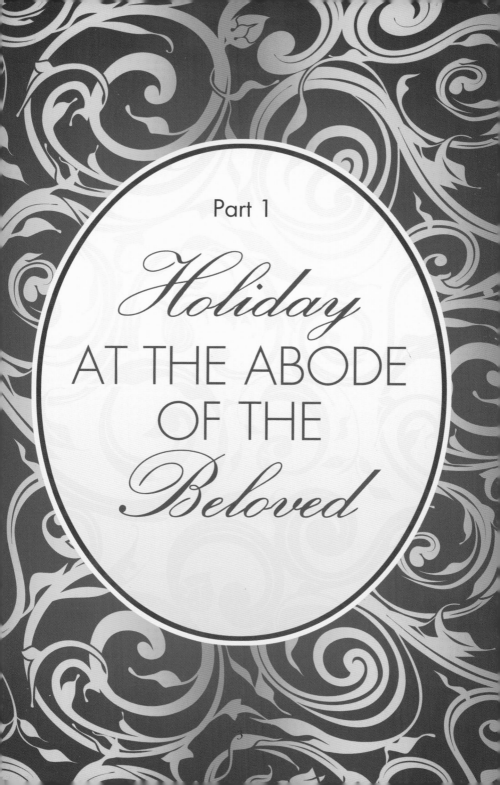

Part 1

Holiday
AT THE ABODE
OF THE
Beloved

Part 1

Holiday AT THE ABODE OF THE Beloved

God is our destiny, and our soul is on a journey back to our divine Home. We are not fully awakened to our blissful nature, which is our soul. Soul is spirit with limitless attributes. How do we connect to our spirit? How do we tread the spiritual path to our true Home? How do we finally progress on the grand divine Highway and experience complete and unadulterated happiness? There is a way. It is an ancient path that begins at the sacred door into infinity of timelessness. It is a threshold that once crossed leads us to experience the Divine. It is God's threshold which leads us to a place of origin, the boundless mansion to which we long to return. The one who holds the key to this door is a spiritual Master.

When we gather in his presence we get bathed in spiritual radiation, making our soul feel at home with itself. We feel calmed and reassured as we are basking in peace and joy. Our soul rests in the soothing presence of Godly love flowing from the uplifting attention of the spiritual Masters, referred in mysticism as "the Beloved." Coming into such a spiritually-charged gathering is coming in the abode of the Beloved. The abode of the Beloved is a gathering in which a spiritual Master helps us focus our attention on our soul. Such an experience is restful beyond words. It is a holiday away from our mundane physical existence.

What makes the holiday at the Beloved's abode special for the soul? In our daily life, our soul is led around by the mind and body, engaging in activities that benefit only our physical and intellectual side, but not our spiritual side. Our soul plays a secondary role to the needs of our body and mind. Thus, the soul is not in its true element and misses out on the unimaginable splendor, exhilarating divine love, and infinite peace awaiting us at the Beloved's abode, our true Home.

Saints through the ages have been frequent travelers to the abode of the Beloved. They want to share that divine journey with humanity. Spiritual Masters have left a roadmap so we also can take the journey to our divine place of origin. In modern times, Masters of the past century, Hazur Baba Sawan Singh Ji Maharaj, Sant Kirpal Singh Ji Maharaj, and the Gracious Master Sant Darshan Singh Ji left a blueprint in the form of their lives, teachings, and writings to show us how to lead our lives correctly.

Every person born into this world grows up, spends his or her life's breaths in a variety of ways, and then passes away. Within that time span, have we ever stopped to consider whether we are fulfilling the purpose for which we are here? How many pass through life without any inkling about where we are going? When we start focusing on questions about the purpose of our existence, our soul experiences an awakening. We start searching for answers. A spiritual Master can give guidance on how to realize the real aim of our human existence and attain our spiritual goals.

Sant Darshan Singh Ji Maharaj was a spiritual Master and mystic-poet saint (1921-1989) who, during his lifetime, put seekers all over the world in touch with the divinity within them. He also left for posterity a treasure house of poetry and poetic prose about the spiritual path. Each of his poems illuminates a different aspect of the spiritual way. One of his ghazals, a type of poetic form in which he wrote much of his poetry, lays out how we can be fulfilled by leading an enlightened life. The following ghazal focuses on how most people are currently spending their lives and what is possible for them to attain. Because many think of themselves as only a physical body, their attention is focused on the world and how to meet their physical needs. Therefore, the bodily needs come before anything else. Saints tell us that when we lead our lives only to fulfill what the body requires, we are not focused on the aspect of life that is more beneficial to our total well being—our soul.

Saints teach that our true existence is not at the level of the body but of the soul. Along with developing our body, we can also spend time in activities that will fulfill our soul. If we only remain at the level of the physical body, then even after leading a life we thought was good, we discover that this human frame will perish. We then realize that only our soul is eternal. Whatever we have done to take care of the body is going to be left behind one day. This ghazal by Sant Darshan Singh Ji points the way to focus on our soul so we can evolve spiritually.

Through the verses of this ghazal, Sant Darshan Singh Ji asks, "Where do we go to get upliftment for the soul?" He also gives the reply, saying, "To the abode of the Beloved." His attention radiating to us when in his presence uplifts our soul to soar from the physical realm through higher inner realms until we reach our real Home, Sach Khand or True Realm.

Many attempt to devote time to spirituality in our homes. We are often distracted by the many chores, responsibilities, and attractions that present themselves at every moment. Yet, by coming to the abode of the Beloved, our spiritual Master, we can bask in the radiation of love pouring out to uplift us. In this book, we can learn from the wisdom of the saints how we can benefit from a spiritual holiday at the abode of the Beloved.

I ATTAINED EVERYTHING, BUT DID NOT MEET THE BELOVED

I won name and fame and all riches of the world;
I attained everything, but did not meet the Beloved.
— Sant Darshan Singh Ji Maharaj

This verse describes how many people spend their lives before they find the abode of the Beloved. Some spend it trying to achieve name and fame, the riches of this world, or whatever other material gains will make them happy. Some work eight, ten, or twelve hours a day to make a living, whether running their own businesses or working for someone else. Most of that time goes into making money to care for their physical needs. From the time they wake up each day until they go to sleep time is spent showering or bathing, brushing their teeth, getting dressed, eating breakfast, going to work, having lunch, coming home, eating dinner, doing chores, or engaging in free-time activities. A point comes when we realize that day after day has passed engaged in these routines of life without meeting the Beloved. The object of our spiritual desires has not materialized.

As we live in society, work, and mingle with others, we also may aspire to attaining name and fame. We may want others to know we have achieved something. Therefore, we may spend time making ourselves look good so others can see we are intelligent, affluent, knowledgeable, or successful in life. The verse states, "I won name and fame and all riches of the world." Yet it also asks, "But what did these do for me?" Nothing, because when we come to the tail end of this existence, our name and fame, our bank balances, and our properties either purchased or acquired in this life are not going with us.

In the second line of verse, Sant Darshan Singh Ji points out what can truly help us. He says, "I attained everything, but did not meet the Beloved." He says that I got everything in this world, but I did not meet the Beloved, the One who could truly assist me and love me unconditionally. The term "Beloved" has two main meanings when used by mystic poet saints. The "Beloved" can mean a spiritual Master or enlightened being who helps us attain self-knowledge and God-realization. In other verses, mystic poets use the term "Beloved" to refer to God. God is the eternal Beloved with whom our soul wants to achieve union. When saints and poets use the terms "Beloved and lover" these serve as an analogy for God and the soul to help us understand the relationship between them. God is the eternal Beloved, and we as souls are lovers of God. Our purpose in life is to love God—nothing else. If we would love God with all that we have—our mind, heart, and soul—we definitely would fulfill the purpose for which we came into this world—communion with the Lord. Spiritual Masters can help us experience that Godly love unfold in our life.

Sant Darshan Singh Ji says in this verse that if we attain name and fame and all the riches of this world, we really have not achieved anything, because we have not experienced the love of the Lord, our eternal Beloved. Many saints say that if we do not meet God, our divine Beloved, then they consider this gift of the human birth to have been wasted. When there are millions of species of life into which we could have been born, we have been blessed to have been born into the human form. Some saints explain that the human form is the roof and crown of creation, because it is only in this form that we have the faculty to attain self-knowledge and God-realization. No other life form can attain spiritual realization. Therefore, the saints impress on us that this human birth is a golden opportunity given to us to achieve the union of our soul with God. Yet, if we do not spend time to achieve that, we have wasted this opportunity. Through the verse, he says that our attention needs to be focused in the proper arena, which is doing whatever we can to reunite our soul with God. If instead we focus only on achieving name, fame, and worldly gains, we have missed the chance to achieve the divine purpose for which we were gifted with a human birth—to know God.

This verse asks us to evaluate whether we have yet met the eternal Beloved. As the revelation dawns on us that our life is passing by without our being with the one who can provide us the true attainment of life, we want to take steps to remedy the situation. For this reason, the poet describes how people may choose to spend their holidays and vacations visiting the abode of a spiritual Master, or Beloved, who can lead them to the Eternal Beloved, or God. Spending time with a Master or Beloved provides a holiday from life's routines that lead only to worldly gains and not to the spiritual fulfillment or bliss of meeting our Eternal Beloved, God, waiting for us within.

Past saints described how they spent every holiday or day off taking a holiday at the abode of their Beloved. For example, Sant Kirpal Singh Ji Maharaj (1894-1974) often traveled by train many hours to a distant city any chance he could to visit his Master, Hazur Baba Sawan Singh Ji Maharaj (1858-1948). As a disciple, Sant Darshan Singh Ji Maharaj (1921-1989) also journeyed from Delhi for many hours by train on Saturday afternoons to see his Master, Hazur Baba Sawan Singh Ji, and return Sunday nights to Delhi to go back to work Monday mornings. When he was younger and going to school, whenever he had an entire summer vacation, he would want to spend it at the abode of Hazur Baba Sawan Singh Ji. Later in life, when Sant Kirpal Singh Ji took over the spiritual work after Hazur, Sant Darshan Singh Ji would go after work and on weekends to visit Sant Kirpal Singh Ji to spend time at his ashram, which was the abode of his Beloved. Many people initiated by either Hazur, Sant Kirpal Singh Ji, or Sant Darshan Singh Ji would have also visited them at their ashrams in India or on tour on each holiday or vacation they had. Why?

When taking a holiday at the abode of the Beloved, we are coming into the presence of a being in which our soul feels at home. In the divine radiation of a Master, we feel intoxication, bliss, and peace. Our soul can relax in the calming presence of divine love flowing from the Beloved's spiritually-charged attention.

Whenever we can attend a spiritual retreat, holiday program, or gathering in the company of a Master, our soul can enjoy divine radiation. To make the most benefit of such an opportunity, we want to put to rest the stress and tension of our work-a-day life that engages us all year round and simply enjoy being in bliss and happiness. We should leave our worries and problems at the door of this venue and treat each gathering at the Beloved's abode as a sacred vacation.

IT SEEMS AS IF
I HAD GLIMPSED YOU BEFORE

It seems as if I had glimpsed you before;
I found signs of this in the realms Beyond.
— Sant Darshan Singh Ji Maharaj

The verse means that when we come to the Beloved's abode, we have a sense that we had glimpsed him before. In this encounter, we feel a recognition. A stirring in our soul tells us that we remember having met the Beloved in the past. Sometimes this realization brings tears of longing to our eyes, and sometimes we are elated with joy. We feel that we know the Beloved. We get this sense because the Beloved is emanating the divine love of God. The soul recognizes it because it came from the region where it used to be merged in God.

We all are drops of God, sparks that emanated from the Divine. The reason we have forgotten God is that our soul is shrouded by our mind and body. When we think we are only the body and mind, we forget we are really the soul. However, when we enter the abode of the Beloved, his divine radiation awakens our soul to its divine nature. We identify with the soul and begin to remember this is who we really are.

Along with this, we awaken to the fact that our true nature is love. God is love, and our soul is a drop of that love. Thus, to reunite with God, we need to develop love for the Lord. Since we cannot see or hear God with our outer eyes and ears, how can we love God whom we cannot see or hear with our physical senses? This is where the guidance of a spiritual Master, or Beloved, is invaluable. Since God is a Power—the Creative Power—it is invisible and formless to us at the level of our outer senses. God is consciousness and can only be realized when we identify with our spiritual state of consciousness.

When we live at the level of our physical body, we are in our physical conscious state. When we identify with our emotions, we are in our emotional conscious state. When we identify with our mind, we are in our intellectual or mental conscious state. How then do we get to our state of spiritual consciousness? The Beloved or Master's role is to put us in touch with our spiritual aspect. He helps us shift our attention from our physical, emotional, and mental consciousness and focus it on our spiritual consciousness.

In this verse, Sant Darshan Singh Ji is telling us that we can attain spiritual consciousness by going on the spiritual journey. This inner journey is one in which we peel off our outer physical layers, emotional layers, and mental layers to find the spiritual gem, our soul, underlying them. How do we get there? We reach the spiritual state by focusing our attention within through a process called meditation. Through meditation, we contact our true nature, our soul, and discover it is one with God, the Source of divine love. The spiritual journey from the physical to the Divine is one of recognizing that our true essence is divine love and the Light of God.

In another verse, Sant Darshan Singh Ji describes it as:

*Wherever I travelled from the earth to the Milky Way,
I found love at every step, and beauty in every glance.*

This journey is one in which the soul travels through inner spiritual regions, each filled with Light, Celestial Music, and divine love. He says that when I went on this journey, it seemed as if I had glimpsed you. When our sensory currents withdraw from awareness of the physical body and collect at the seat of the soul, located between and behind the two eyebrows, we are uplifted into the regions Beyond. We have an inner eye, called the third eye, single eye, *divya chakshu, ajna* or *aggya chakra, daswan dwar* or tenth door. Through the guidance of the Master Power, our third eye is opened so we can experience inner Light and Sound. By concentrating our attention within, through the grace of the Master, we can withdraw temporarily to this eye-focus. Through a spiritual boost from the charged attention of the Master, we can go from the physical realm to the astral realm, from the astral to the causal realm, from the causal to the supracausal realm. Transcending these three lower realms, under the control of the Universal Mind, the layers of mind, matter, and illusion covering our soul are removed. We shed our physical, astral, and causal bodies one by one. In the supracausal realm, we arrive at a landmark called the Mansarovar, a pool of nectar where, after our physical, astral, and causal layers had been stripped away, we experience in wonder that we are soul. At this stage, our soul cries out "Sohang," or "I am That." We realize, "O Lord, I am of the same essence as You." Yet, our journey is not over, as our soul is still covered by a thin veil of illusion. From the supracausal realm, we ultimately reach the purely spiritual realm, called Sach Khand, meaning the true

14

Home or true Region. The thin veil that surrounded us in the supracausal realm is removed, and we realize our true essence as soul. In Sach Khand, we merge in God, the eternal ocean of all bliss, happiness, and divine love. We have finally fulfilled the true purpose of our human birth. We discover that we are not only a part of God, but also one with God. At this stage, we realize that we had glimpsed God before, ages ago, when we were originally one with the Lord. We have finally come Home.

Our soul was originally a part of God in Sach Khand, but we forgot our true nature. As our soul separated from God to inhabit the different realms of creation, it was encased in the different layers or coverings. As we began to identify ourselves with those coverings and those other existences, we forgot the source from where we came. Only when those layers are peeled off do we realize we are soul. Sant Darshan Singh Ji says in this verse that as we undertake the spiritual journey, we experience that we have seen the Beloved before, because the layers that separated us from that Power have been peeled off.

Tremendous grace is showered on us in the company of a saint. When we receive his spiritual glance, our soul recognizes it and we are transformed. There is an interesting incident from the life of Hazur Baba Sawan Singh Ji Maharaj. A man was on the platform of a train station, while Hazur was riding in a train. For a split-second, the eyes of that man met the eyes of Hazur, who was looking out the window of the train, giving the man the sweet darshan of the Master. Many years later, when that man, who was not initiated by a Master, was on his deathbed, he told his family surrounding him that a saint was appearing to him. He described the figure of Hazur Baba Sawan Singh Ji. One person with him, who was initiated, recognized that the one being described was Hazur—the same person the man saw for a split-second riding in the train years before. Hazur was coming to meet his soul at his time of death to help him cross into the Beyond. You can well imagine the gift we receive when in the presence of the Master. Just think how that one split-second glance of grace at a train station to a man not even initiated by Hazur was enough for the Master to appear to him at the time of his death to help him. In this way, the Master would take care of his soul so that his karmic accounts would not be in the hands of Kal, the Sustaining Power, ruling over the three lower regions. The Sustaining Power practices "tit for tat," where for every thought, word, and deed we commit, we either are rewarded or must suffer the consequences. Instead, his karmic accounts would be in the hands of the Master, who practices the law of compassion and mercy and has the power to wipe clean our past sanchit karmas. The Master takes us off the wheel of transmigration and brings our soul back to God in the highest spiritual realm of Sach Khand. We have no idea of the amount of grace afforded to us by these great Masters, both in their presence anywhere and in their spiritual gathering. In their company, our soul recognizes that glance and our lives are forever changed.

On the spiritual journey, we realize we are connected to God. This is why Sant Darshan Singh Ji says, "It seems as if I had glimpsed you before." During our life, our attention is focused on the outer world. However, as we go on the spiritual path, we start to get a glimpse of the Lord. The inner travels make us realize who we really are, that we are part of God, and that we can experience God. He says, "I found signs of this in the realms Beyond," meaning that we had glimpsed our connectedness before—not in this world, but in the regions within.

To love God is to meditate. This is the secret to experience the love of the Lord. Sant Darshan Singh Ji, in laying out where we are, where we need to go, and how we can get there, says we can reach God by meditating. In meditation, we need to find the radiant form of the Master who serves as our guide on the inner journey. When we withdraw our attention, we find inner Light. By absorption into that Light, we ultimately come to the radiant or ethereal form of our spiritual Master, the Beloved. This radiant form of the Master takes us on the journey from the physical to the astral, causal, and supracausal realms until we reach the highest spiritual realm, where our soul merges in God. We then realize we are one with God.

Whenever we attend a spiritual holiday program or meditation retreat, we can maximize our progress by putting in time for meditation so we can realize that we have glimpsed the Beloved before. When we go within, we have an actual experience of being one with God. The proof is in seeing for ourselves. When we meditate, and leave behind all our worldly troubles and problems, an inner field of vision opens up for us and we behold the Master's radiant form in all its glory. Its beauty and radiance is not merely a sight to behold, but also it bathes us in Godly love that attracts us further within. This pulls the soul from its attention on the world and its problems to enjoy the inner regions that are free of pain and sorrow. We can truly relax on a spiritual holiday when we go within because we reach regions beyond the lower realms of suffering to bask in the eternal sunshine of realms of bliss, peace, and joy.

I MOVED STEADILY TOWARDS THE ABODE OF THE BELOVED

Although there were many obstacles along the way,
I moved steadily towards the abode of the Beloved.
— Sant Darshan Singh Ji Maharaj

As we start following a spiritual path, others may ask us, "Why are you a vegetarian?" or "Why do you spend time meditating and closing your eyes when there are so many other active things to do?" Some may ridicule us because we are doing something different than they do. Other difficulties may occupy our attention, such as a financial crisis, in which one job is not enough. We may have to work two or three jobs to make ends meet. Physical, emotional, and relationship problems may trouble us. Our loved ones may have health problems. Sant Darshan Singh Ji says in this verse that although there are many obstacles along the way, I moved steadily towards the abode of the Beloved.

There are many examples of what others have gone through to reach the abode of the Beloved. Some traveled thousands of miles. Others struggled to get vacation time or days off from work. People have found ways and means to overcome all those obstacles. How many times has it happened that our boss did not want to grant us leave for a vacation, but somehow we managed to work it out so we could get time off anyway? How many times have we become ill but decided we wanted to go to a satsang or spiritual gathering, so we got up and went anyway and found that by attending, we happily discovered that all our sickness was gone? Sant Darshan Singh Ji alludes to the fact that life does bring difficulties, but when our attention is on finding God, we are not burdened even by undergoing those challenges. Although many obstacles came along the way, he moved steadily towards the abode of the Beloved.

How do we move steadily towards the abode? Zeal and passion are required to reach there. We need to put in an effort. What is that effort on the spiritual journey? Our effort is putting in at least the minimum of two and a half hours daily in meditation. Along with meditating regularly, we also need to lead an ethical life.

To reach the abode of the Eternal Beloved within, the realm of Sach Khand, we have to overcome many difficulties. The biggest obstacle is our mind and its attraction for the temptations of the world. We have to still our mind so it will let us meditate. The mind concocts many reasons to keep us from meditating. It coerces us to ignore the call of the soul to focus within and instead spends time in the outer enjoyments of the world. Even if we sit for meditation, the mind does not let up. It occupies our attention with thoughts of the past and future.

In whatever field we engage, we may look at those who achieved success and wonder why we are so far behind them. We may admire those who top our field and think they reached there by luck. We pray to God to give us the same luck so we can also excel.

Even in the spiritual field, we hear or read about those who found God. If we also yearn to find God but have not yet done so, we wonder how others have achieved it. We wish the hand of luck to be placed on our head so we can also know God. What we fail to realize is that success is not based on luck; success comes from diligent efforts to reach one's goal.

To illustrate this, there is an example from history from the life of a king of England. The king had four sons. The three older boys were strong, but the youngest was a smaller, thinner lad who lacked their strength.

In those days, books were rare. The few books that existed were hand-written by pen or painted by brush and were beautifully written and bound. They were extremely costly and not made for the masses.

A rich person happened to give a book to the king and queen. The queen wanted to show the book to her four sons. She called them to her chamber and pulled out the rich volume. Since books were rare in those times, few knew how to read. The mother showed the book to her four sons, even though they did not know how to read. She pointed out to them the strange letters handwritten on each page. The children admired the book as they had never seen one before, but they could not understand what the strange letters on the pages said.

As the four boys admired the book, the mother said, "Even better than the way the letters decorate the page is the story it tells. If you would learn to read, you could enjoy the story. I will give this book to the first one of you who learns to read."

The youngest boy asked the mother if she would give him the book.

She said, "I will give it to whoever is the first to learn to read. If you come first in that contest, then you will definitely have the book."

The oldest son said, "Who wants to read? I would rather play."

The second oldest son also said, "Who wants to do reading? I would rather look for wild birds."

The third oldest son agreed, saying, "If I were going to grow up to be a monk, then I would learn to read. However, we are not going to be monks. We are princes of a king and will become princes. We should not waste our time."

The youngest son said, "I really want to know the story in this book."

A few weeks later, the youngest son returned to his mother and with a broad smile said, "Can I look at that book again?"

The mother took it out of a locked cabinet where she kept her precious belongings and handed it to her son. The boy opened to the first page, holding the book with great care. He then read the first word on the page. He kept reading aloud the story in the book perfectly. He did not make a single reading error.

The mother was astonished and asked, "How did you learn how to read?"

The boy said, "I went to the monk and asked him to show me how to read. I had a lesson every day for the past few weeks. It was not easy to learn what sound each character made and to combine them into words. The monk said I can read really well now!"

The mother was delighted. The other boys had crept into the room to see what was going on and listened as their younger brother read aloud.

They began to taunt him for learning to read. One of them

said, "So we will be princes when we grow up, but you will only be fit to be a monk!"

The mother ignored their comments, picked up the book, and handed it to her younger son, saying, "You have won the prize. The book is yours. Do not worry about whether you will be a king or a monk, for whatever you do, the gift of reading will make you wise and noble."

His mother's prophetic words came true, and the boy grew up to the one of England's wisest and noblest king, known as Alfred the Great. Among his accomplishments was to encourage education.

This anecdote illustrates how we have to put in an effort to reach our goals. The young prince chose to achieve something and stuck to the goal, even if others taunted or criticized him. He chose a goal that was not easy, but which led to gaining knowledge. Taking a detour off the beaten path that others chose to walk, he did not mind hearing their critical remarks. He found a way to achieve success through hard work. He also found a teacher who could help him reach his goal. Then, he spent day after day learning how to read to see what wonders lay in the book. Persevering for hours and hours, day after day, he finally mastered his skill. With joy, he claimed his prize and the wonderful world of knowledge it opened for him.

We have a similar challenge as the prince had. We have chosen to understand a book that few know how to read. We are attempting to understand the book of life, which offers answers to many mysteries unknown to the masses. Through this book of life we can learn why we are here, where we came from, where will we go after this life ends, and is there an Author who wrote the book of life. The reading of the book of life does not involve our outer eyes and ears. To understand the book of life we need to go within through meditation and discover the eternal story within. The young boy's task was to read letters on a page. Our spiritual task is to close our eyes, gaze at the inner Lights, and listen to the inner Sounds. Through diligent effort of looking and hearing within, we will also learn the true story, the story of our soul and God. We will be able to rise above the consciousness of this physical body and world to witness glorious inner worlds of beauty and Light. The story that unfolds for us within is the soul soaring through higher and higher realms of existence. We will discover the astral, casual, and supracausal realms, until we ultimately come to the realm where abides the Author of the book of the mystery of life, God.

The boy did not learn to read through luck. He achieved his goal through finding a teacher and putting in hard work. He stuck to his studies for many hours, day after day, until he achieved success. This is what we need to do on the spiritual path. We can seek the advice from an experienced teacher who knows the method for us to find God. Then, when we find a teacher who can get us to our goal, we need to do our lessons. We should not think that everything comes by luck. Seventy-five percent of what we do is through our karma, which means our thoughts, words, and deeds accumulated from the past. However, twenty-five percent of our life is free will. With our free will, either we can go in a direction that is Godly or we can go in a direction that keeps us in the cycle of transmigration and karma, where all our thoughts, words, and deeds bring us again and again to this world. According to the law of karma, whether it is good or bad karma, we have to come back to this world to reap the rewards and the consequences of our past. We need to get off the wheel of transmigration to return to God. For that, we need to put in an effort. The lessons for finding God involve meditating on the inner Light and Sound. It is not a one-time effort—we need to put in at least two and a half hours minimum each day, day after day, month after month, year after year. By this steady diligent practice, we will find God.

A spiritual gathering or holiday retreat provides us time to perfect the art of reading the book of the mysteries of the Beyond that can only be read with our inner eye through meditation. With the same diligence applied by the youngest prince to learn how to read outer books, we too can be diligent in our meditations to read the inner book of the mysteries of the soul and God through meditation. Only then will we attain what others who have gone before us have reached. We realize it is not luck but commitment that moves us to our goal. We can begin from today to take diligent steps toward God. Let us meditate each day, for two and a half hours daily, with loving concentration and attention. If we persevere, we will attract God's grace for an extra boost within. In time, we too will be successful and win the ultimate prize, union with God.

A coal miner once discovered a plant growing in the coal mine. The seed had germinated in the bottom of the mine. Normally, such a plant only grows six inches. However, this plant had grown one hundred twenty feet to reach the light above it. Think of what obstacles the plant had to overcome to reach the sunlight. It overcame its own limitations as a short plant to do what it had to do to survive. If a plant can put in that effort to grow from six inches to one hundred twenty feet, we should be able to put in an effort to get to our goals and rise into the regions Beyond. Similarly, our growth should move steadily toward the inner Light even though insurmountable obstacles may come in our way.

Sant Darshan Singh Ji says in this verse, "I had the zeal and passion that even though there were big storms, difficulties, and problems along the way, I did not let them deter me. I still kept on going toward my goal." The key is to keep the goal of the Beloved's abode always foremost in our minds, hearts, and souls. If we are clear about the goal, then we will not let anything interfere with our regular meditations. We will make it a point to sit for meditation each day. We will also realize that if we spend our meditation time by sitting and thinking of other things instead of gazing within free of thoughts, we are wasting our meditation period. Rather, we should do the concentration accurately and reserve all thoughts for other times of day. We should protect our meditation time so that nothing disturbs it.

In the worldly sphere, when we go to meet our worldly beloved, nothing can stop the lover. The lover often scales tall mountains, crosses rough seas, and travels long distances without food and rest to rush to the arms of the beloved. Nothing can deter the lover from reaching the beloved's door. For a beloved, it can truly be said, "An obstacle is something you see when you take your eyes off the goal." Thus, lovers do not see obstacles.

It has been poetically said that if the home of the Beloved was in the middle of the ocean, or if the path to the Beloved's abode was filled with hundreds of snakes, ferocious tigers, and lions blocking the way, or if even the angel of death was obstructing the path, a lover would still not be deterred from walking on the lane to the Beloved's abode. Nothing can stop a lover from reaching the abode of the Beloved.

Let us all move steadily towards the Beloved's abode. There

we will find the Beloved waiting. All our trials and tribulations will fade away and we will be lost in the bliss of union. We will overcome the setbacks and obstacles and proceed with Godspeed on the journey. May we all have the strength to overcome all obstacles so we can find the peace and bliss in the Beloved's abode.

FORTUNATE IS ONE
WHO FINDS YOUR THRESHOLD

Fortunate is one who finds your threshold;
Why should one search for another threshold?
– Sant Darshan Singh Ji Maharaj

This verse says that once we have found the right way and are traveling on the spiritual journey leading to God, it does not make sense to waver. The search for the way took time, effort, and energy. We searched and searched and finally found a pathway to reach our spiritual goals. However, once we have found that road but keep searching, we deplete all our energy, time, and effort, which instead could be better used to take us further toward our goal.

Once we find something helpful for us, we should stick to it. The verse says that they are the fortunate ones who stick to their goal. There are seven billion people in the world. Very few of them undertake this spiritual journey. However, if we search for a way to reach God, then once having found it, we should not waver. Just as Alfred the Great went to a monk who taught him how to read, similarly, we can find an enlightened being, a spiritual Master, to guide our soul back to God. Once we find the right way and receive guidance, we should not waver.

Sant Darshan Singh Ji tells us that we do not have time to

lose. We all have limited life spans, whether sixty, eighty, or one hundred years or more, but one day we all physically have to leave this world. Once we find the right way, let us firmly travel on it. He says, "Fortunate is one who finds your threshold; Why should one search for another threshold?"

It is only when we reach God that we are satisfied. The soul will not stop until it returns to God. It is like a fish trying to swim upstream to its origin. The verse says there is no need to search for any other threshold once we find God. God, the Source of all wisdom, love, and bliss, fulfills all the soul's desires. Once having found the Lord, all the gifts of the world lose their attraction. Everything of this world pales into insignificance once we reach God. After all, the world is but a reflection of a reflection of a reflection of the Lord. When we have the real flower, who needs artificial ones?

We had God, but exchanged the Lord for the temporary pleasures of this world. The verse says that once we regain God and return to the Lord's lap, we should not seek any other, but stay forever in God's abode. The key is to find the right roadway that will lead us to God. We can prolong our journey or we can move along at supersonic speed. We need to ask which roadway is the most direct to the Lord's door.

We should not trust in blind belief. We need to have actual proof of the competency of the path we choose to go back to God. This comes in the form of inner Light and Sound, an experience of going within, or the divine appearance of our spiritual guide. Once we find a threshold in which we receive proof, then the verse asks, why search for another? When we reach God, then we find the fulfillment of our soul and will have eternal peace, happiness, and love.

If we attend a spiritual retreat, let us make the best use of that time. That involves meditating, going to satsang, doing selfless service, and basking in the divine radiation flowing to us. This means we need to prevent our mind through its thoughts from leading us from one threshold after another. Instead of focusing on the abode of the Beloved, the mind can lead us to its own abode filled with worldly thoughts and desires. If we go to a spiritual gathering, we can benefit more if we stay focused on the Beloved's abode and not on the mind's abode meant to distract us. We can leave aside any desires the mind puts in our path and instead stay submerged into the divine love of the Beloved flowing to us. By doing so, we will find our true holiday in bliss at the abode of the Beloved.

MOMENTS OF PEACE AND SOLACE IN THOSE GLANCES

*Where can Darshan find moments of peace and solace
But in those glances for which he has been searching
his entire life?*
– Sant Darshan Singh Ji Maharaj

This verse describes the peace and solace we receive from the glances of God either directly when we attain God-realization or when we see them reflected through the darshan or glances of a saint or Master. Eyes are the pools through which spiritual radiation flows, giving us peace and tranquility.

To soar into regions Beyond, we need to be in a state of calm and quiet. Sant Darshan Singh Ji says there is a difference between the temporary peace and solace in this world and the permanent peace and solace from coming in contact with God.

We want peace in our homes, in our community, and in the world. If there is no peace, it bothers us and we are in turmoil. We may find moments of worldly peace by sitting in nature, in the quiet of our home, in being with families or friends, or in doing something we like. We may find solace in looking at majestic mountains, listening to the waters of a babbling brook, or smelling fragrant flowers in a garden. We may find joy in spending quiet moments with loved ones or pursuing a hobby.

However, all those moments are transitory because life is a series of interruptions, with ups and downs. Each day brings us new challenges from financial, health, or relationships problems. Whatever moments of peace we enjoy are temporary in this world.

Permanent peace comes when our soul reunites with God. We realize that our true connection is with God and that the world is but a passing dream. When we identify our self with this world, we suffer the ups and downs of life. However, when we identify our soul with God and stay consciously connected, we are always in peace. This peace stays with us, even in the midst of trials and tribulations. We are bathed in God's love at all times. Until then, we are like the man in the story of "Footsteps in the Sand." A man noticed that whenever he was connected to God and felt God's presence, he saw two sets of two footprints, or four footprints, in the sand, However, in times of his greatest need, he noticed there were only two footprints in the sand. The man complained to God as to why God had forsaken him as there were only two footprints instead of the usual four. God revealed to him that the reason there were only two footprints was that during those times of great need, he was being carried on God's own shoulders. Similarly, God is upholding us, but we remain unaware and ignorant of this fact. We can become aware by meditating so we can realize that God is within us and with us at all times.

The glances of a Master reflecting God's love give us a boost towards experiencing the eternal peace waiting for us. Those glances come from being in the abode of the Beloved. It uplifts our soul and pulls us into the inner realms. Sant Darshan Singh Ji praises these glances because they carry with them the spiritual radiation that uplifts our soul back to God. The glance is like a magnet pulling iron filings towards itself. The soul cannot resist this attraction. It suspends its interest in the world because it receives so much more love through those glances.

That glance catapults us in meditation to the still center, or eye-focus, where we contact the Light and Sound. Such a divine glance pulls our sensory currents from awareness of the body and concentrates them at the single eye. When fully concentrated there, we see and hear God's inner Light and Sound. By absorption in the Light and Sound, we meet the radiant form of the Master. His glance is intoxicating and pulls our soul higher until we cross the astral, causal, and supracausal regions and finally reach the throne of God. There, we get the glance of God in its full glory and merge in God. Then, there is no one to give the glance and no one to receive the glance because the two become one. In that moment, we are filled with more bliss, intoxication, and love than we could ever dream possible. We are lifted from the world of time and space to live in eternity.

The glances emanating from the Master Power help us know ourselves as we truly are as soul. They uplift us from the physical to the Divine, so our soul can meet, experience, and merge in God. Then, the purpose for which we came into this world is fulfilled.

When we attend a spiritual holiday at the abode of the Beloved, we have many opportunities to share in experiencing the Divine and enter states of tranquility. We have many chances to meditate in the early morning, afternoon, and evening and better understand the spiritual path.

I pray each who attends a spiritual gathering receives glances of grace for which we have been searching so we can go on the inner journey to reach the abode of the Beloved and be showered with eternal bliss and love.

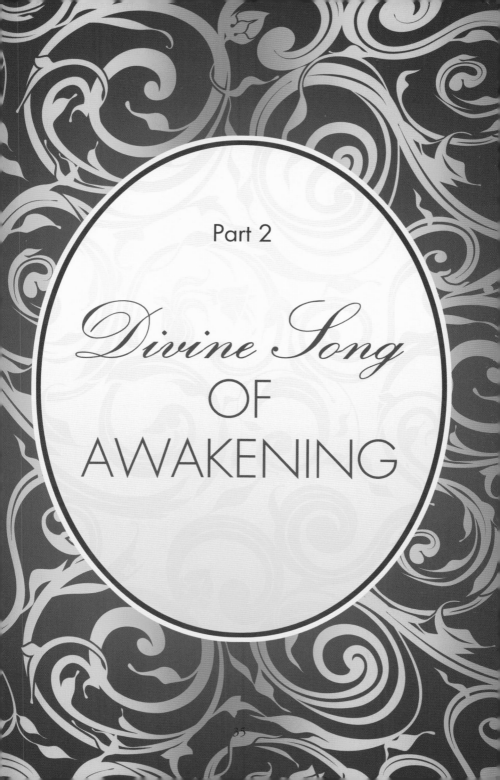

Part 2

Divine Song
OF
AWAKENING

Part 2

Divine Song OF AWAKENING

ON HEARING YOUR DIVINE VOICE

All salutations to the Lord of the tavern!
All salutations to the Lord of the tavern!
Your call has awakened the slumbering centuries,
On hearing your song, the heart has taken wing
*   and begun to chirp,*
On hearing your divine voice,
*   your mad lover is in ecstasy.*
*   – Sant Darshan Singh Ji Maharaj*

The poetry of Sant Darshan Singh Ji Maharaj is so rich that each time we read his verses, we find new meaning, often related to what is currently happening in our lives. The words of the great saints are never dated. Every time we read and focus on them, whether written recently or thousands of years ago, they provide truth and guidance as to how best to spend our life. They make us aware of where to focus our time and how to reach our goals as rapidly as possible to achieve fulfillment.

In each person's life a moment comes in which we have a transcendent experience or a revelation making us aware that we have a higher purpose in this world. Suddenly, amidst the daily rituals of waking up, getting dressed, going to work, eating, and sleeping, we glimpse that there is something more to this life. That moment may come when we are a child, a teenager, a young adult, or an adult. Some may not have it until their senior years of life. Whenever it comes, it leaves us transformed. For example, if there is a death of a close family member—and the closer they are to us the greater the impact—a realization sets in that this physical life is temporary. Suppose we have a traumatic experience, such as during a medical checkup the doctor tells us we have a terminal illness, we start thinking about life and its meaning. We might read a spiritual book or poem which has such an impact on us that we start thinking about life's purpose. We might be in the presence of a saintly person and suddenly find ourselves in more ecstasy and joy than we ever had before. Many kinds of experiences can transform us. Suddenly, we question who are we, why are we here, where do we go when we die, and what is our purpose in life. Once these burning questions arise, there is no turning back. We are restless until we find the solution. In this poem, Sant Darshan Singh Ji addresses the moment when we awaken to these questions and set out on a quest to find their answers. He undertook the spiritual journey to union with God through the grace and guidance of his Masters, Hazur Baba Sawan Singh Ji and Sant Kirpal Singh Ji. Thus, his teachings, books, and poetry describe these spiritual experiences and show us how we also can reach states of eternal ecstasy.

The first line says, "All salutations to the Lord of the Tavern!"

This refrain plays like background music to the entire poem. It expresses gratitude to the one responsible for the seeker's awakening and ultimate enlightenment. Sant Darshan Singh Ji drew heavily from mystic poetry for his images. The Lord of the Tavern does not refer to someone who works in a bar; rather, it refers to a divine Cupbearer, or one who puts us in touch with God. In a worldly tavern, wine is served, but in the spiritual Tavern, the Cupbearer pours out spiritual Wine of God, in the form of Light and Sound that leads our soul back to the Lord. This poem is a celebration in which the seeker is grateful to the Cupbearer for these Godly gifts of divine love, Light, Celestial Music, and ecstasy.

In this verse, Sant Darshan Singh Ji talks about a spiritual gathering called a satsang, in which we are in the presence of a Master or Cupbearer, who gives us a transcendent experience of God. The fluttering of our heart and soul when we are touched by the love of the Divine cannot be described in words. In a satsang, spiritual radiation penetrates through layers of mind, matter, and illusion, stirring our soul. This uplifts our soul from the physical to the Divine. We are in rapture, joy, and ecstasy unlike any we have ever known before.

In this verse, Sant Darshan Singh Ji describes the benefits of going to a satsang. What does satsang means? The word "sat" means "truth," and "sang" means "to be in the company of." Thus, "satsang" means "to be in the company of truth." Satsang is a gathering where seekers after truth learn a method by which they can attain direct firsthand experience of knowing themselves and realizing God.

Mystic poets take examples of this world so we can understand spiritual truths. In this verse, Sant Darshan Singh

Ji uses the analogy of a worldly tavern, a cupbearer, and wine to describe a spiritual Tavern, a divine Cupbearer, and Godly Wine to convey the benefits of being in a satsang.

For example, a tavern in the outer world is a place in which people go to drink. Some drink to get away from the difficulties of the world. Others drink to feel intoxication, while some do so because they are addicted and cannot give it up. In a tavern, there is a cupbearer, called a bartender in the West, who pours out drinks. That analogy of the cupbearer and the tavern has been used for thousands of years, where today people refer to that concept as a bartender and a pub or bar. People go to a tavern to be intoxicated, oblivious to their surroundings, or in a state they think will make them happy, not realizing all the side effects, hangovers, and difficulties drinking liquor, beer, and wine bring. A tavern is also a place where people go who have no prior connection with each other, such as where strangers gather from different religions, countries, and backgrounds yet amicably sit together and drink. That example is used in this verse describing what a satsang is and how a satsang is a community or arena in which all kinds of people come. There are rich and poor people and educated and illiterate people. There are people who are followers of one faith and those whose faiths are entirely opposite in beliefs. There are people of one culture or another. The satsang is open to one and all.

The divine Wine refers to a current of the Light and Sound of God, a contact with which fills us with divine intoxication. In the satsang, there is a Cupbearer. The Cupbearer refers to the spiritual Master who serves the divine Wine to seekers after truth. All types of people come to the satsang to experience the divine Wine. We want to experience the spiritual Nectar so we can be in a state of Godly intoxication not only for a short time but also for all times to come.

In the life of Guru Nanak Dev Ji Maharaj, the king of the times invited him to his palace. As was the tradition, the king offered him a glass of wine. Guru Nanak graciously refused the wine, beautifully saying that he does not want to drink that wine because its intoxication lasts only for a few hours and results in a hangover and other difficulties. Instead, Guru Nanak Dev Ji wanted that Wine that is spiritual because its intoxication stays all twenty-four hours of the day—all night and all day—and lasts forever. That spiritual Wine is the divine Light and Sound of God, the holy Word, or the Naam or Shabd that we experience when we go within during meditation. In the satsang, we are put in touch with the spiritual Nectar flowing through the Master, who doles out cup after cup of that divine Wine.

This verse, in which salutations are offered to the "Lord of the Tavern," expresses the gratitude for the benefits that seekers receive from the Cupbearer or spiritual Master in the spiritual Tavern or satsang. They imbibe the divine Nectar, Shabd, Naam, or holy Word poured out to them. The verse says that I pay obeisance to the Lord of the Tavern, to the Master Power, to the one who transforms our soul and reunites us with God.

The gratitude expressed in this verse shows the recognition a seeker has when put in touch with the divine Power of God. Why is the poet imbued with such great gratitude? Most people pass through life searching for something, but are not aware of what it is. We know we are missing something, but do not know what. Thus, most of our activities or search seems to focus on finding the missing piece of our life only at the physical level. For example, if we evaluate what we do all day, we see that we spend time waking up, taking a bath or shower, and getting ready—getting ready for what? For most people, they get ready for going to work or raising a family. Since we will be busy engaged in that for many hours, what do we do? We eat breakfast. It is interesting that during the night, most people do not eat, which is like having a fast for about eight hours, and we want to break that—so what do we do? We eat breakfast, a word derived from "breaking" a "fast." When we wake up, we want to break that fast. With what do we break it? With delicious food. Some may have toast and jelly, some may have rice cakes and avocados, some may have *idli* and *sambhar*, and some may have potato *paranthas*. We break it with whatever we think would taste good.

Then, we get dressed and go to work. We may do manual work, mental work, or a combination of both. Then, we have lunch at work, whether we eat at our place of work or go out for lunch in a restaurant. Then, we feed the body again. It is a machine and it needs fuel. The body is like a car in which we put in gas and it runs. We have to fill the tank periodically, depending on how far we go. If we go only ten or twenty miles, we might fill it up once a week. If we go two hundred miles, we might have to fill it up every day. It is the same with the body. Needing fuel, we eat lunch and later snack a bit. When we come home, we have dinner.

At the end of the day, we feel tired so we relax. The tension we created for ourselves all day long by doing this thing and that, meeting this person and that, causes us to feel the need to rejuvenate, whether we watch television, use the computer, or do whatever else we enjoy.

Finally, we get ready to rest the body. The body needs rest, just as you cannot run an engine twenty-four hours a day, day after day. It will work for a few days, but then it goes "clunk" on you. The same with the body—it needs rest.

Then, the next morning, we awake, break the fast, and go through the same routine. In all of those activities, we have tried to keep this body well. It gets hungry, so we feed it. It gets dirty, so we clean it. Along with the making money to pay the cost of our basic needs to survive physically, we also try to fulfill the desires of the mind by buying whatever else we think we need. There are many attractions in the world and we spend time working to earn money to pay for them. While in this cycle, time passes. From a young adult to an adult, as we engage in this daily routine in caring for our body and mind, life passes by quickly.

Sant Darshan Singh Ji repeats the line, "All salutations to the Lord of the Tavern" because repetition in any poetry emphasizes a point. He stresses that it is a privilege to have been picked up from this routine life and placed in the Tavern of the divine Cupbearer, or the satsang of a Master, where our soul can connect with God.

In the next line, Sant Darshan Singh Ji explains, "Your call has awakened the slumbering centuries." What does this mean?

Before our awakening, it is as if we are sleeping. Sant Darshan Singh Ji has rightly used the term "slumbering centuries." We think we are only sleeping during this lifetime, but our soul has been asleep for centuries. How did our soul enter this slumber? Our soul started out in the lap of God. When God separated particles of Itself called souls and sent us out to inhabit creation, we became lost in the attractions of the world and forgot our true Home. Thus, we are in a state of slumber or forgetfulness that we are soul. We think we are the mind and the body. We forget our true essence is the soul, as a part of the Creator.

As we identify with the mind and body, all our attention goes into their development. We focus our life on taking care of our body and attending to the wishes of the mind. We ignore the needs of our soul. Let us look at our own lives and make a list of where we spend our time. A good portion of our day goes into our body: eating, sleeping, dressing, bathing, doing our hair, grooming, sports, exercise, dieting, and working to pay for clothing, shelter, and medicine for our body. Then count how many hours we spend attending to our mind. If we have a mental job, we use our mind at work. We focus on the desires of the mind by entertaining it with television, radio, movies, computers and digital devices, the Internet, talking to or texting people, socializing, or exploring hobbies. Thus, by the end of our life, we have worked hard to have a well-maintained body and a well-developed mind. However, where do we stand when it comes to our soul and our spiritual life? How much time daily do we spend on that? Most people either go to a place of worship once a week or during certain holidays. We may pray to God, but are we mostly praying for something that is going to help our body, our mind, or the people we love? How many times do we pray to God for God? Thus, before we get the call of awakening, we may devote more time to the body and mind than to the soul.

At some point, we get a call of awakening from God. It is like Prince Charming awakening Sleeping Beauty. When the call comes, it awakens us from centuries or lifetimes of living life in a state of slumber.

The call of awakening may come in many ways. It may be a

moment when we face an impending disaster. We may be in a car accident or find we have an illness when we think our life is going to end. Suddenly, our life flashes before us and we realize that everything we did and everything that we accomplished is not going to help us as we approach the unknown beyond this life. It may be that we suffered the loss of someone we love. Maybe the awakening comes through something we read that makes us think about our existence. For some, it may come through a friend telling us about their quest, which awakens a longing in us to also take that journey. God has many ways to reach us.

This line of verse has a deeper meaning in the original language in which it was written than in its English translation. One loses the true meaning when translated, because there are no words accurately to convey the original words. The original word that means "your call," also means "the Sound," referring to the "Sound Current," or "Light and Sound of God." Every time we read Sant Darshan Singh Ji's verses, we find so much depth that we wonder why we did not think about this meaning before. Many meanings are embedded in one verse. Here, he is describing how the Master Power works. Our soul is encased in our body. The soul also has a mind, whose role is to keep the soul away from knowing God. However, the soul is a part of God, which is reverberating within each of us. God and the soul are within us, but the soul is not aware of God. When God was One and wished to be many, there was a vibration that resulted in two primal principles, the Light and Sound. This Light and Sound current created and sustains all creation. As it emanated from its Source, it brought into being various realms of creation, including this physical realm, with all the stars, suns, moons, planets, this Earth, human beings, and all forms of life. This vibration of Light and Sound gives life to all living forms. It reverberates within us at all times. When we invert our attention to connect to that inner Light and Sound, we can travel on that current back through all the realms of creation to merge back in the Source, God.

Through the connection to the Power of the Light and Sound, we can be one with God. However, the mind keeps the soul from connecting us with that Power by distracting us. When we have a sincere desire to know God, we are put in touch with someone who can connect us to the Light and Sound within. The Master comes to our aid by teaching us a meditation technique by which we can invert our attention to find the Light and Sound within us so we can travel back to our Source. He connects us through his charged attention to the Light and Sound. Then, to keep our mind from distracting us, he gives us a technique called simran, or mental repetition of the five Charged Words. By repeating these five Charged Words, our attention focuses on the Light and Sound of God, the Naam, or Shabd. Then our soul is uplifted from the physical to the astral, causal, and supracausal realms to reunite with God in the spiritual realm of Sach Khand. The Master serves as a catalyst connecting the soul with the Power of God within us through giving us a contact with the inner Light and Sound.

Sant Darshan Singh Ji says that it is your inner "Voice" or "Sound Current," meaning the Light and Sound of God, which takes us out of this slumber and puts us into the state where it is awakened. When the soul realizes itself as soul and that it is a part of God, it starts to have an inkling of its true purpose. Then, the soul wants to know God and even develops a passion to unite with God. That is that first spark that the Master ignites in our soul to enlighten us.

The next line of this verse tells us what happens when we get that call: "On hearing your song, the heart has taken wing and begun to chirp." This describes what happens to us when we get the call of awakening. Something familiar resonates in us. We feel like we suddenly recall something that we have forgotten for a long time. This song may reach us in many ways. For example, while reading a book about God and the soul, suddenly tears may spring to our eyes. It is as if we suddenly remember our true Home. Maybe while listening to music, the sweet sound of a flute, a violin, or a harp moves us to tears. There are certain sounds that may remind us of a much higher music we once heard. We may meet someone in tune with God and suddenly find in his eyes something strangely familiar. We feel a great peace and solace in that person's presence. When our soul suddenly recognizes someone whose soul has merged in God, it wants to leap with joy.

The verse describes how the heart takes wing and begins to chirp. This line is using the image of a bird chirping with happiness. We often hear the expression, "Happy as a lark." It is a poetic way of describing supreme happiness. The heart feels like it starts to soar like a bird. It is actually not the happiness of the heart but of the soul. The soul has been imprisoned in this body and mind in a state of forgetfulness for centuries. It cries to be heard. However, we are sleeping. The soul is waiting for a chance to be awakened so it can be freed of its imprisonment. When finally the moment of awakening comes, the soul is in ecstasy. It is let out of its cage. The soul is in joy and ecstasy. When we tap into the soul, our whole being—our mind, body, and soul—are all drenched in joy and bliss.

In this verse, the poet refers to "Hearing your song." This is more than just a figurative expression. The word "Song" needs to be taken literally. It is actually a Song or an inner Music that we hear. It is the Music of God, or the Music of the Spheres.

One of the gifts we receive from a spiritual Master is our connection with the divine Light and Sound. The stream is radiant Light and celestial Music. The Music is so captivating it pulls our soul's attention from this physical world and sweeps it into the lap of God. It is hard to imagine how powerful the inner Music is since we think of music as being the songs to which we listen on the radio, I-pods, I-pads, or digital devices, or in a live concert.

Sant Darshan Singh Ji used to say that outer music can take us to the end of this physical universe. To go beyond that, we need the Music of the Spheres.

What is the "Song" being spoken of when he writes in the verse, "on hearing your Song"? He is referring to the celestial Music. When our body and mind are stilled we can see and hear the divine current of the Light and Sound of God. On hearing your divine Song, another name for the divine Light and celestial Music, the heart takes wing and begins to chirp. As our soul hears the divine Song, it becomes as happy as a lark. It is so joyous that it reaches a state of ecstasy because it is experiencing its divine Source. It starts to realize the state of separation it was in for centuries and centuries and enters a state of reunion. Sant Darshan Singh Ji says that on the wings of that celestial Music, or connection with the divine Light and Sound of God, the soul rises from the physical to the spiritual regions Beyond.

To understand the power of the inner Music, think of the

effects outer music has. Music of this world has a tremendous effect. When we listen to music, whether it is the beautiful voice of a singer, the sweet sounds of instruments being played, or its melody, tempo, rhythm, or beat, we become entangled. Some listeners shake their heads or tap their feet on the ground. The intoxication in the music holds our attention. Here, in this verse, he says that on hearing your sound the heart has taken wing and has begun to chirp. By taking the example of a bird or a lark who chirps with happiness, he is describing our state when we connect with the divine Song.

A story about a king illustrates how music can affect us. In his kingdom, he discovered a great musician. Hearing about the singer, the king called him to the palace and liked his talent. As the singer was excellent, the king had him regularly perform for him. Being the king's musician added to his popularity and soon, people from neighboring kingdoms heard of him and also invited him to perform for them. The musician asked the king for permission to perform in other places as well, and the king let him go. He went on a long journey from one kingdom to another. Wherever he went, the singer was paid handsomely, collecting much money and many expensive treasures. After awhile, he became homesick and wanted to return home.

The musician found a ship leaving for his kingdom and booked a seat. He brought on the ship all the money he earned and the gifts he received. After the ship set sail, it encountered huge storms and rough seas and was waylaid. The ship was blown so far off course, the sailors and passengers did not know if they would find their way back on track.

As the difficulties of the voyage increased, the captain and sailors became obnoxious to the passengers. The captain once had been a pirate and somehow landed a job as the captain of the ship.

One day, the captain and the sailors discussed the musician who was onboard. The topic arose about how wealthy the musician was from all his performances in the other lands.

The sailors said, "We are so far out at sea. Why don't we rob the musician since he has so much money with him? We can get all his wealth before we reach land."

After agreeing they would rob him, they asked the captain how they could get away with this crime.

The captain, being an unscrupulous man, said, "That is easy. We will take his money and throw him overboard. We are so far from land. When we get back, if anyone asks where he is, we can say that he fell overboard when the ship was rocking from the storms. In this way, he cannot report us to the king."

As the sailors and the captain spoke, they did not notice the musician approach outside their closed door, about to enter to talk to the captain. When he heard them talking, he stopped and did not open the door to the captain's quarters. He secretly listened to their conversation through the closed door and heard they were plotting to kill him. He trembled with fear.

In a panic and not knowing what to do, his first impulse was to plead for his life.

He threw open the door to the captain's quarters and said, "I heard what you are saying. Look, instead of taking my life by throwing me overboard, just take my money. You can have every bit of it, if you only spare my life."

The sailors had already made up their minds to do away with him. They feared that if they spared his life, he would report them to the king.

The sailors said, "We will not spare your life. If we get back and you tell anyone, we will be in trouble. However, we will give you two choices. You can either be slain by a sword or you can die by jumping overboard. Which one do you choose?"

The musician gave it quick consideration and said, "I will jump overboard, but please give me one last wish to fulfill." He knew it was a tradition that if someone was in jail and sentenced to be put to death he or she would be granted one last wish.

The captain asked, "What is your last wish?"

The musician replied, "I want to sing for all of you. Allow me to sing you one of my best songs. I promise that as soon as it ends, I shall jump overboard."

The sailors said, "Oh, this is great. We heard you are a great singer. We are bored anyway and have nothing better to do and we can finally hear your talent. Okay, you can sing for us. But, as soon as your song is over, you must jump overboard."

The musician told them, "Before singing, I first want to get dressed up for you just as I do in the big theaters." They agreed to let him get dressed up properly for the performance. He went to his cabin and took his time in getting dressed. He then went out to the front deck of the ship to sing.

The captain and sailors stood around him as he prepared to sing.

He chose a string instrument which had a wooden base with the strings pulled across it. He began playing his instrument and singing along. He sang so melodiously that the sailors were captivated by his beautiful voice. They began humming along and became intoxicated. Some were even moved to tears as he played his sweet song. They had never heard anything so beautiful in their lives, but their greed for his money far exceeded their appreciation for his talent.

The musician sang and sang and sang for hours on end his unending song. It was the longest song they had ever heard. Another hour passed by. Then, yet another hour went by. They did not know when he would stop, but they did not mind as this entertained them for the many hours of their journey to get back to their homeland. They did not interrupt him, as one never stops a musician in the middle of a performance.

He was still singing when the beautiful colors of the sunset spread across the sky. He kept singing as twilight turned to the starry night sky. He kept singing until dawn burst. They were captivated by his music and let him go on.

Suddenly, he stopped singing, turned towards the front deck, and jumped overboard. Relieved that he was gone, the sailors and captain raided his cabin and took all his money.

A short while later, they realized he had kept singing until he had sighted land. They assumed that this fall into the water would have killed him anyway.

When the ship docked, the captain and sailors were surprised to see the king's soldiers there to greet them. They asked him if they had seen the musician, as they had heard he was returning home on their ship. The captain and sailors denied having him on the ship and lied to them, telling them he had stayed back in the other country.

However, the soldiers knew they were lying because the musician had thrown himself overboard near enough to land to swim ashore. They knew he had sung until he saw land and then jumped. Unbeknownst to the sailors, the musician had swum to shore and rushed to the king's palace to tell him what had happened.

The king's soldiers had received an order to bring the captain and the sailors to the king. The captain and sailors were brought in and the king asked them where the musician was. They said they had not seen him, but they had heard he was staying in the other country.

At that point, the king told them he knew they were lying and produced the musician who was kept hidden in the other room. The captain and sailors were arrested, the musician's money was returned, and the musician was free and alive. This story shows that the power of music was able to keep the sailors entranced long enough for the musician to save his life. He had kept singing and singing long enough to reach the safe haven of his homeland.

Just as the power of outer music could save the musician's physical life, inner Music can save our soul.

This is the message Sant Darshan Singh Ji conveys in this verse. He says, "On hearing your song, the heart has taken wing and begun to chirp." When we listen to the divine Song— the Music of the Spheres—and are connected with the inner Light and Sound, we are uplifted into the regions Beyond. That journey brings us to our true abode, the lap of God, or Sach Khand, the region of all Truth. That connection with the inner Light and Sound comes through the grace and guidance of the Lord of the Tavern, the Master Power.

The world outside is complicated. As children, we think everything is simple. However, as we grow up, we find that problems with our relationships, our work, our finances, and our health, and turmoil in our communities and the world seep into our lives. Realizing that life is not as rosy as we thought it was and that we have to deal with problems, we seek guidance.

As children, we take guidance from teachers at school. At work, we take guidance from those with whom we work or our coaches and mentors. For daily life problems, we take guidance from people in our neighborhood. We need help to pass through our life properly. However, the inner regions are vaster than this physical world and much more complicated. If we do not have guidance to travel through the inner realms, we can be waylaid. Just as in this world, there are people to oversee towns, cities, states, and countries, there is a power overseeing the three lower regions, called Kal, or the Sustaining Power. Within these three lower regions—the physical, astral, and causal realms—Kal lays out many distractions for us by which we can be easily caught. Just as some countries have laws preventing emigration of its citizens to keep its population under control, so does the overseer of the three lower regions want to prevent souls inhabiting them to emigrate from them to enter the spiritual regions beyond the three lower realms. The guidance of the Master Power helps us to rise beyond the three lower realms to reach our ultimate goal in the highest realm of Sach Khand, the purely spiritual region in which the soul can reunite with God.

A spiritual Master can guide us from the physical realm, to reach all the way to Sach Khand, the realm of all-consciousness. However, without a spiritual Master who knows the journey and can guide us like a travel agent to the realms beyond the three lowest ones, we can only reach as far as the teacher whose care we are under can take us. If our teacher has only gone to the second realm, we can only go there. If a teacher has only gone to the third realm, we can only go there. However, a spiritual Master who has travelled to Sach Khand and knows the way, can take our soul all the way to our true Home. This is where the salutations to the Master come in. It could take aeons and aeons and centuries of slumbering and great difficulty to rise beyond the three lower realms because there are so many distractions along the way. Those people who find a Master, like Hazur Baba Sawan Singh Ji Maharaj, Sant Kirpal Singh Ji Maharaj, and Sant Darshan Singh Ji Maharaj who were Masters of the past century, are extremely lucky because their help can guide souls to their ultimate goal.

This story of the musician illustrates how the grace and guidance of the Master, the Lord of the Tavern, works by putting us in touch with the heavenly Music of the Naam or Word, the Light and Sound of God, which can save our soul. The captain who is after us is the Sustaining Power governing the three lower regions that does not want us to reach our safe haven of Sach Khand, the true abode, where God resides. Kal is after our true wealth, which is our soul, and wants to raid our spiritual wealth by claiming us as its own. In this way, we do not look for God, and thereby leave Kal's domain.

A Master gives us the connection to the inner Music. As long as we are connected to the Naam or Word, Kal cannot sidetrack us. When we are initiated, we are given that link to the divine Light and Music. Thus, Kal cannot come near us to entangle our soul. Just as the sailors were unable to touch the musician while he was singing, Kal cannot touch us while we are immersed in the Music of the Spheres, the current of Light and Sound. Initiation gives us that link so Kal cannot waylay our soul on its journey back to God.

Meditation keeps us engrossed into the Light and Music of the Spheres. When we meditate, we practice two methods: one is meditation on the inner Light or simran practice, and the other is meditation on the inner Sound or bhajan practice. In meditation on the inner Sound, we sit in stillness and listen to the heavenly strains reverberating within. We stay absorbed in the variety of Sounds that come to us within. By absorption into these celestial Melodies, our soul rises on the current and rides on it until it reaches its Source, Absolute God.

By staying absorbed in the heavenly Music, we are not entangled by distractions placed in our way by Kal. The practice of listening to the Sound Current can lift our soul so we can attain union of our soul with God in this lifetime.

Sant Darshan Singh Ji beautifully expresses this experience in this line of verse: "On hearing your divine voice your mad lover is in ecstasy." The voice to which Sant Darshan Singh Ji refers is the Music of the Spheres, the Light and Sound of God. How can one who has heard this divine Melody describe it to one who has only heard music of this world? How can the hearing describe sound to one who is deaf? All we can do is use pale analogies. If we think of the most beautiful music we have ever heard in this world, it still does not compare with the music known as the voice of God. Some people feel happy and full of life when they hear rock n' roll music. Others feel uplifted when they hear classical music. Some feel moved by rhythm and blues. Some people prefer soft music. We may feel touched by the music of our homeland or our country's national anthem. Certain instruments of this world may make us feel inspired. If we put together all the best experiences of music we have heard of this world, they are nothing compared to the Music of God that we can hear in meditation.

Why? First, the Music of God is not made by any instruments. It is a Melody that reverberates from God. Thus, it is the Source of all outer music. Outer music is but a reflection of a reflection of a reflection of God's inner Music. Second, the Music of God is like a magnetic current that lifts the soul onto itself and carries it with it into the spiritual realms. Once we contact that Sound, our soul is uplifted into the Beyond. That Sound fills us with indescribable ecstasy. We are so intoxicated that every pore of our being is crying out in ecstasy. It is an ecstasy greater than any we can have in this world. Again, think of the most beautiful experiences in this world. That is still pale compared to the ecstasy of our soul contacting the Light and Sound and traveling to spiritual realms within.

Once we have a taste of this, we become, like Sant Darshan Singh Ji says, "mad lovers." A mad lover means one who is so intoxicated and drawn to the Beloved, he or she cannot get enough of the Beloved. We become so passionate to be with the Beloved because of the ecstasy we receive. We want more and more of that bliss.

Those who have been in love recognize how much happiness there is when we are in love. In love, everything beautifies. Everything is right, joyous, and beautiful in love. Everything is in ecstasy in love. That is the state we attain when we experience the divine Light and Sound within.

Those who go within and experience the divine Light and celestial Music have a connection with that spiritual conscious Power that puts us into everlasting bliss.

This poem by Sant Darshan Singh Ji describes how the seeker has moved from awakening to achieving the realization that we are soul and a part of God. The proof comes from contacting the inner reality in the form of the Light and Sound. However, the seeker has received much more than he or she has bargained for. The seeker has not only received a taste of divine knowledge and the answer to the spiritual questions, but is receiving ecstasy, bliss, and happiness.

The seeker is grateful to the one who has answered his or her questions and bestowed upon him or her divine intoxication. The seeker has now turned into a lover because he or she has realized the great gift the Lord of the Tavern has given. Because this divine Wine of God's love and the Light and Sound provides so much more than anything material in this world can give, the seeker turned lover wants to partake of it again and again. This is why they appear to be mad in love with the Giver. It is in such a state of gratefulness to find the reality within that the seeker cries out the refrain of this verse:

All salutations to the Lord of the Tavern!

TOUCHED BY YOUR
DIVINE GRACE

The Cup is filled as it moves among your tipplers,
Touched by your grace, the world
*   has come into its own,*
May I, too, receive my portion of your intoxication?
All salutations to the Lord of the tavern!
All salutations to the Lord of the tavern!
*   – Sant Darshan Singh Ji Maharaj*

In this verse, Sant Darshan Singh Ji expresses a prayer to the Lord of the Tavern. The poet sees the tavern filled with many tipplers. They have all come with cups they wish filled with the divine Wine of ecstasy. The poet is in awe of how every person who comes has a full cup. Each cup, no matter what color, what size, or what shape is filled. The Cupbearer seems to have an endless supply of divine Wine of God. No matter how many tipplers come, they all get to drink until their thirst is quenched.

The poet also notices that all cups are filled. The Cupbearer does not care if our skin color is dark or light, or whether our eyes are blue, brown, green, or black. The Cupbearer does not care if we are rich or poor, literate or illiterate. The Cupbearer serves all equally. Just like tipplers when drinking do not care if their companions are of the same religion or nationality, similarly, in the tavern of the Lord, all are equal, and all are served God's love to their fill.

Notice that the verse says that the whole world has come into its own. The Cupbearer does not come for people of one country. The Wine of God's love is for the whole world. The Cupbearer's job is to pour out without end so that the whole world may drink. He gives it lovingly to all who are thirsty.

Sant Darshan Singh Ji in all humility now beseeches the Cupbearer to pour out the divine intoxication to him as well. He is anxious lest the Cupbearer pass him by. He is also waiting for his share of intoxication. He is hoping the Beloved gives him a portion, as he knows how painful it is when he is not in contact with the divine Wine, the inner Light and Sound. He knows how excruciating separation can be from the source of Godly love. He does not want the intoxication to end, so he prays to the Lord of the Tavern to make sure he receives his portion.

The story of the seeker now becomes the story of a lover of God. Once we taste the divinity within, we become mad lovers who want it again and again. We are grateful to the Lord of the Tavern for the gift. Then we start to pray to the Lord of the Tavern to keep the Godly Wine of the Light and Sound current flowing in our direction. We know that the more divine Wine of God we drink, the more we want. The more we want, the more effort we put into our spiritual practices. The more effort we put in, the more the spiritual progress and we receive more and more inner Wine. As we progress spiritually, our cups increase in size. We require more and more of God's love. The more we get, the more we want. The more we want, the more we get, until ultimately our cups become like the infinite ocean of God. The cup becomes an ocean of love, Light, Music, and bliss.

Spiritual teachers are always there to help us find the inner hidden treasures. They are calling to us all the time. We do not believe or listen to them, until we are ready to receive their call. Then, through our own experience, we have our awakening. Once we receive it, then we know its value, and we too will praise their gift, as Sant Darshan Singh Ji says:

All salutations to the Lord of the Tavern!
All salutations to the Lord of the Tavern!

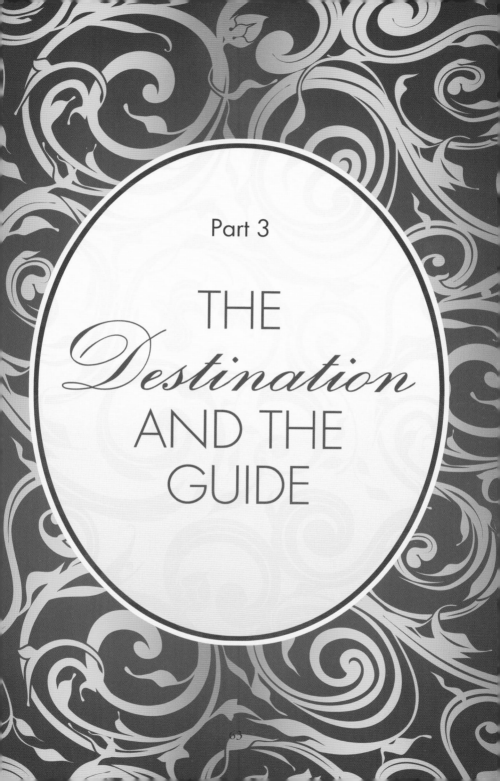

Part 3

THE
Destination
AND THE
GUIDE

Part 3

The Destination
AND THE GUIDE

THE DESTINATION, THE GUIDE, AND THE WILL

When we are in distress, we call on you,
It is you, your devotees pray to and revere,
You are the destination, you are the guide
and the will that impels us.
All salutations to the Lord of the tavern!
All salutations to the Lord of the tavern!
– Sant Darshan Singh Ji Maharaj

Ups and downs are a part of life. It is rare to pass through life without some problem. We face many situations that bring pain and anguish. We must deal with physical illness and unexpected accidents. In the world of finance—sometimes we have money and sometimes we must do without. We suffer the loss of loved ones when a relationship does not work out, a child moves away, or a parent or relative dies. We must endure many disappointments, as our desires are not fulfilled. Even the act of entering the world in childbirth is a painful experience. At times, we feel we are succumbing to our difficulties.

When things are going well for us, we rarely think of God. However, the moment we face some hardship or pain, our thoughts turn immediately to God for help and assistance. Sant Darshan Singh Ji describes this state in another verse of his ghazal. He explores the benefits of having a spiritual Master during those times. Through this next verse, he explains what we gain when we pray. When we pass through a difficult period we may pray because we have tried everything else we could to fix our situation, but it is not being resolved. Sometimes our prayers are answered, and sometimes they are not. There are times that despite all our prayers, our situation does not seem to change for the better. These times may cause us to doubt if God actually exists. We wonder, "Why hasn't God answered our prayer?"

This verse addresses the issue of looking for help when we are in pain. It also expresses the blessings and benefits of having a spiritual Master. It praises the Lord of the Tavern, the Cupbearer or spiritual Master, for the wondrous way he helps us through our difficulties in life. In our times of distress, we can call to the Master for help.

The help we get from the Master Power in solving our problems is unimaginable. In a previous verse, Sant Darshan Singh Ji Maharaj offered gratitude for the benefit of being in the satsang arena or "Tavern," where we are in the presence of the Master and receiving guidance to reach our spiritual goals in this lifetime. In this verse, he provides another reason for offering "salutations to the Lord of the Tavern." There are many examples of people who had physical ailments or difficult emotional or mental situations who then wrote to the Master, saw the Master, or conveyed a message to him. Within a matter of a few days or weeks, or at times right away, they found the difficulties were either totally gone or they received tremendous help to deal with that situation better.

When we call on the Master in distress, how does the help work? We all have karmas. The karmic account must be wound up for our soul to return to God. On our own, it may take countless lifetimes to pay off the balance. The biggest load of our karma is the sanchit karma, the collection of all the karmas accumulated as we pass through our many previous lifetimes. Out of that sanchit karma, the part apportioned for this life is called the pralabdh karma. Those are the karmas we pass through in this lifetime. We also all create karmas on a daily basis, called kriyaman karma. Every day we have thoughts, words, and deeds.

When a Master initiates a disciple, he dispenses a special grace. The load of our sanchit karma is taken over by the Master Power at the time of our holy initiation. That is the biggest load we have. Those sanchit karmas are wiped away by the Master Power as we are initiated. The Master Power can take care of the pralabdh karmas, too, but if those pralabdh karmas were wiped out, we would have no karma left. This means there is nothing left to pay off, so this life would be over. For this reason, the saints do not touch the pralabdh karma at the time of initiation. They leave those for us to pass through as part of this life. For this reason we go through the highs and lows of life. The pralabdh karma that is supposed to be played out in this lifetime is not touched by the saints. However, when these difficulties come in our life, then the Master Power helps us unburden it. It is like when a child is in pain, the mother or father help to relieve the suffering. When the child is in the lap of the parents, he or she feels secure so that his or her pain lessens or goes away. Similarly, the Master Power, filled with compassion, helps us.

The law of karma is the law of judgment, based on "an eye for an eye and a tooth for a tooth." The law of judgment says that if we do good things, we are rewarded, and if we do bad things, we face the consequences. However, the Master Power works under the law of compassion. Like a parent, he cannot bear to see the disciple suffer. Thus, he may at times soften the karmas by taking them on himself. The disciple then finds relief for his or her pain. Then, since the karmic debt must be paid, the Master must suffer that debt on his own physical body. That is why we sometimes find the Masters undergo great pain. These are not karmas of their own, but they are taking on the karmas of their disciples.

To illustrate this, there is an anecdote about a judge who lived in France many years ago. He was considered a fair, but kind judge. One day, a case was brought before him in the court. A baron who leased apartments brought a lawsuit against a poor widow who rented an apartment from him. She had missed a payment on her rent. When she did not pay, the landlord tried to enter her apartment to evict her, but she did not permit him entry. Thus, besides evicting her, the landlord was bringing a suit against the woman.

When the case was brought before the judge, he found there was a clause in the agreement written in small print saying the landlord had the right to enter the premises of any property he owned whenever he wanted, even if someone were renting it. There is usually something written in small print in a contract, which most people do not read, and even if they do, many people do not even understand the legal terms in which it is written.

The judge realized that the woman could not have known about the clause because it was in fine print and in legal language with which she had no familiarity.

When the judge realized that legally the landlord's case was strong, he asked the baron to be lenient with the woman, saying, "She is a poor widow. She did not purposely try to block entrance to you to her house. She also is undergoing hard times. Why not be compassionate with her? Do you have to be so merciless with this poor woman?"

Nevertheless, the landlord was hard-hearted and refused to give up this case against the woman, saying, "No, no, no. I want the rent. I want her to undergo the penalty. I also want her to pay for the legal fees." Knowing that according to the terms of the contract, the woman was wrong to forbid entry to the landlord, he was broken-hearted about having to give his judgment. He had to abide by the law, but he did not want to see the woman hurt by losing her place to live and paying a fine, which he knew she could not afford.

Again, the judge tried to reason with the landlord saying, "This woman did not intentionally try to break the law in violating her contract. She has not financially tried to bring harm to you. Can't you give up this lawsuit?"

The landlord was not only heartless, but also stubborn. He refused to let go of this case.

The judge had to abide by the law and rule against the woman, agreeing she had violated the terms of her contract and would have to pay the penalty. The penalty was to pay the missed rent and the cost of violating the lease plus the legal fees of the lawsuit. As he announced the verdict, tears came to the judge's eyes realizing this would be difficult for the woman as she did not have the money. He was bound by law, but his heart went out in compassion for the woman's plight.

The order proclaimed that her apartment was to be seized, along with her belongings, according to the contract terms.

The woman broke down and cried, saying, "O God, if You are merciful and righteous, You would be a friend to the widows and helpless orphans."

The judge descended from his chair to go to the lady, and knowing that he could not change his verdict, he put his hands into his pocket and pulled out his wallet. He then counted out his money and presented to the woman the costs that she had to pay for the penalty, court costs, and the rent she owed. This gave the woman enough money to pay off the lawsuit and to be able to stay in her apartment.

The woman was moved to tears at the generosity of the judge. She could not believe that he would do this for her, being a stranger to him.

She then said to the judge, "Thank you so much for your kindness and generosity. How much time do you want to give me to pay you back for this financial help?"

The judge beautifully replied, "When my conscience tells me that I have done the wrong thing in giving you the money to help you!"

She knew this meant that as a judge he had to make that judgment, but he did not want to be paid back, as his conscience and compassionate nature compelled him to help relieve her of that difficulty, and that in his heart, this was not an improper thing to do.

His generosity was widely known throughout his city as a leading example of blending fairness with compassion. Such examples help us understand how the spiritual laws work. Just as this judge did, spiritual Masters work according to the law of compassion.

There are two laws working in creation. One is the law of judgment and the other is the law of compassion. As we navigate life, we find most of it is governed by the law of judgment. The physical region is part of the three lower realms of creation in which the law of karma, based on the law of judgment, prevails. Yet, Masters are governed by the law of compassion. They care about us, they love us tremendously, and they want us to reach our goals. They realize we are going to pass through difficulties due to our own past karmas, yet, out of compassion, they often take over our difficulties themselves.

There are historical examples of Masters of Sant Mat going through a painful time because they have taken over the karmic loads of their disciples. Once Sant Darshan Singh Ji Maharaj was with Sant Kirpal Singh Ji Maharaj and he noticed that when he was trying to pick up a cup of tea, his hand was shaking. It is difficult to see your Master in trouble, so he looked at him and tears came to his eyes.

Sant Kirpal Singh Ji said, "Darshi (his nickname), why are tears coming to your eyes?" Sant Darshan Singh Ji remained silent, as he rarely spoke in the presence of Sant Kirpal Singh Ji but would listen. Sant Kirpal Singh Ji then said, "Darshi, don't you know I just initiated many souls on the inner realms?" Through that comment, we see how the karmic loads are taken over by the Master Power so that our loads are unburdened. That is how help comes to us. On one hand, they know we must pay off our karmas according to the law of justice. Yet, they can offer help to us. They do so in several ways.

First, they take over our karmic account at the time of initiation. They know we committed the acts that resulted in these karmas and that we are supposed to pay for them. However, as a benefit of receiving initiation into the Light and Sound, they take over our karmic accounts so that our sanchit karmas are burned up.

Second, they can reduce our pralabdh karmas by taking some of our burdens on themselves. They are agreeing that those karmas must be paid according to the law of justice, but the law of compassion moves them to take over some of them on their own physical bodies to lessen our load.

Third, they also instruct us in a way of living that reduces our accumulation of kriyaman or daily karmas. They ask us to lead an ethical life of nonviolence, truthfulness, selfless service, love, humility, and purity, so that we do not accumulate more daily karma. In this way, because we live a clean, pure life in which we did not accumulate any more karmas, we have no karmas left to pay when this life ends.

We are fortunate to have such great Masters who are filled with compassion like the judge in the story. Although the Masters abide by the laws of the three lower regions, they find loopholes to help us. Like the poor widow in the story, we are ignorant. We do not read the clause of our life contract and make many mistakes. We ignore many of the laws that govern this world, such as the need to be nonviolent, truthful, pure, humble, and selfless. We think we can ramrod our way through life, breaking the rules of the universe, and never have to pay for it. We remain ignorant of the law of ethical living. However, the Lord of Judgment is recording everything and presents us with our own lawsuit at the end of our life.

The Masters are compassionate and know that as humans we are bound to commit mistakes. Thus, they take mercy on us. While allowing the penalties to be presented to us, they find ways to help us. If they feel we will benefit and learn from paying a penalty so we may improve, then we may pass through those karmas. If they feel that it is too great a burden, they may choose to lessen our karmas by taking it on their own selves. They also give us another out. If we meditate accurately and become absorbed into the Naam, the Light and Sound of God, our karmas are also burned off. Thus, meditation on the Current of Light and Sound has the added value of reducing our karmic load.

While the Masters are governed by the law of compassion, they ask us to take compassion on our own selves. We can do so by spending time in meditation. They can help us but up to a point. We have to take responsibility also for meditating so we can burn off our own karmas. They exhort us to meditate daily for two and a half hours, not only to be able to rise above physical consciousness to soar into the inner realms to reunite with God, but to burn off our karmas quicker. Let us also be compassionate on ourselves and meditate regularly. We are then helping the Masters to help us, and we will find our path in life is easier as our karmas are being lessened and we can soar back to God.

There is an account describing how one disciple of Baba Jaimal Singh Ji wanted him to initiate a friend into the meditation on the Light and Sound. Baba Ji replied that he would rather initiate hundreds of other people than that one. He explained that the man's karmas were so heavy that it was not yet time for him to be initiated. The man insisted, and out of compassion,

Baba Ji gave in. After initiating that man, the man's karmas were so great that Baba Ji had to take some of them on his own body. Baba Ji returned to his home and was extremely ill for several weeks, taking the burden of that man's karmas. It was only then that the man realized that to have his friend initiated, his Master would have to suffer the man's karmas.

The Masters generally do not tamper with our pralabdh karma, but when the disciple cries out to him with all his or her heart and soul, the Master cannot ignore it. Out of love and compassion, he responds and often lessens the karmas of his disciples. There are also some disciples who do not want to pray to the Master to lessen their karmas because they love him so much they do not want him to suffer for them. However, the Master is like a parent, and even unasked for sometimes the Master helps us through our difficulties.

These examples of how the Master takes our karmas on their own selves illustrate how we only see the Master as an outer physical being; we do not see the spiritual activity happening within and through the Master's physical frame. The Master Power works in ways that are unimaginable to any one of us. How does help reach someone who is thousands of miles away? It is difficult to put into words and understand this help at the intellectual level. We only can have a glimpse of what we see or hear with our outer eyes and ears, or what we or those close to us experience. When it happens to us, or someone close to us, we realize that it has truly happened.

It is important to note that Masters do not come to create miracles; their job and duty is to help us reunite with God. One of the responsibilities of the Master initiating us is to make sure our soul returns to its true Home. They help our soul get there, irrespective of who we are, from what cultures we come, or what is our background. Each has to reach the goal of being one with God. The Masters provide the help we need to reach there.

A disciple is always seeking that help from the Master. This is why Sant Darshan Singh Ji says in this verse, "When we are in distress, we call on you," whether the call comes through a prayer, through writing a letter whether we mail it or not, through a physical interview where we can talk about our difficulty, or through someone else conveying the message. Those are various means of trying to get the message from us to the Master. We call out because we realize his help will take care of our difficult situation.

When Sant Darshan Singh Ji says in the next verse, "It is you, your devotees pray to and revere," he is talking about disciples who realize that the Master Power can help us return to God. When we are only aware of our physical, mental, and emotional states, we are unable to experience God, as to do so we need to rise to a state of spiritual consciousness. Disciples recognize that to transcend into regions Beyond, we need help. If we could have risen by ourselves, then we would not be on the wheel of transmigration and would have been back with God by now. Yet, we are not there, so we need help and guidance, which we receive from the Master Power. This is why the verse says, "It is you, your devotees pray to and revere." When devotees realize that all the help they need can come through the grace of the Master, they begin to revere and love the Master. As they pray to and receive guidance from the Master, they realize that no one else in the world thus far has given them that kind of guidance to reunite their soul with God. They know that in life they have received guidance for their physical and mental development from teachers and mentors who taught them about their body and mind, but no one else had yet helped them reunite their soul with God as the spiritual Master is able to do. When that realization sets in, they become grateful to the Master for that spiritual help.

In the next line of verse, Sant Darshan Singh Ji says, "You are the destination, you are the guide, and the will that impels us." Therein lays the whole path of Sant Mat. The path of Sant Mat tells us repeatedly that our soul and God and the way back to God, which is the divine current of Light and Sound of God, are all one and the same. The Master Power expresses itself as the current of Light and Sound that brought all creation into being and sustains all life. God, the soul, and the Light and Sound current are all one. They are spirit. They are Light. They are love. They are consciousness. They are bliss. They are the same. The destination is God. The guide is the Power of God manifesting as the Light and Sound of God with which the Master connects us. The will that impels us is the attention of the Master Power that propels our soul into the Beyond and back to God. The disciple in this verse is realizing that they are all the same. The Master Power working through the Master gives us the impetus to return home through his attention. The Master Power working through the Master guides our soul on the inner journey back to God. The Master Power is the same as the God Power, waiting to receive us when we reach our destination and our soul merges back in God. Our soul is a part of God and is conscious. The Light and Sound is our connection that our soul has with God. We need to travel on this divine Light and Sound to return to our Source. If we could understand that our soul, God, and the way back to God are the same, and that the one who puts us on the way back to God is the Master Power, because on our own we cannot be connected, then the whole path of Sant Mat would become simple and straightforward to comprehend.

What is the meaning of the "will that impels us" mentioned in this verse? The will that impels us is the pull that comes from the Creator. Love emanates from the heart of the Beloved. Sant Darshan Singh Ji used to explain that we think that we love the Beloved, but unless the Beloved first loves us we are not in the position to love the Beloved. The Beloved loves us, God loves us, and the Master Power loves us. We reciprocate that love as a lover to the Master Power and to God. Therefore, the will for us to know God comes from God. Since at our own level we are unable to experience God, we experience it as a Power coming from God that radiates to us through the vehicle of a Master. Many people are under the wrong impression that the Master is the body. The Master is not the body; the true Master is the spiritual Power, called the "Master Power" working through that vessel. The Master has merged into God and can put us in touch with the Light and Sound already within us. It is that Master Power and not the physical form of the Master that gives us upliftment when we are in his presence. It is also that Master Power that helps us through times of trouble.

When we pray to the Master, we are not actually praying to a human being, but to the Power of God within him that is also within us, except we do not recognize it until we meditate and go within. It is that Master Power that helps us. When we receive initiation from a spiritual Master, he is duty bound to take us back to God. Part of the duty is to take over the karma of the disciples to lighten our load so our soul can rise into spiritual realms. As karma is the account of all our thoughts, words, and deeds, both good and bad, accumulated through all our lifetimes, we have to pass through them. Since there is so much to pay off, and as we pay some off, we accumulate more, that balance sheet would never come to a zero balance. Therefore, out of compassion and to help lighten our load, the Power of God burns up all the sanchit karmas from our past lives. Only the pralabdh karmas, which are the portion of the sanchit karmas allocated for this life, are left for us to pay off in the remaining days of our life. If these karmas were burnt up also, our life would end because we would have no more karmic debts to pay here. The Master leaves the karmas allotted for this lifetime as these must be paid. We also must pay off the new karmas we create as we live our daily lives. This is why he exhorts us not to create any new karmas.

Sant Darshan Singh Ji is saying, "You are the destination, you are the guide and the will that impels us." The will that impels us is that Power that pulls us to itself. The Power of God is radiating to us through the human frame. That human frame is a physical body like us—it talks, it lives in this physical world with us, and it eats with us, so we can relate to it. The guidance comes through the human frame, but it is the Power within that frame that is the real Master that radiates to us and uplifts our soul into the realms Beyond—it is not the body that is the Master doing that. The will to return to our true Home comes through that frame. The Power working through that frame is like a magnet that attracts our soul in the direction of God. That Power is the Power of God. Therefore, when we are pulled to the Power, we are actually being pulled to the Power of God.

It is the Master who becomes the guide, helping our soul reach God. Why do we need that help? We need assistance because our attention, which is the outer expression of the soul, is scattered in all directions in the outer world. It is thinking about what is happening with the basketball game, the stock market, or what sales are going on in the stores, pulling our attention in all kinds of directions and fragmenting us. Some of us are going here, some of us are pulled here, and others are pulled there. What does the Master Power do? It pulls our attention to focus on God. That is the work of the guide. That is why the verse is saying, "You are the destination and the guide, and the will that impels us." It is the love of the Lord that impels us towards God. The guidance comes from the Master Power.

The first phrase says, "You are the destination." What is Sant Darshan Singh Ji trying to tell us? In history, we have examples that give an inkling of what the Master Power is. There is a classical example of a queen named Indu Mati. She became a disciple of Kabir Sahib. As Kabir Sahib initiated her and she received more of the blessings, she was transported on the spiritual journey within. She rose from the physical to the astral realm, from the astral to the causal realm, from the causal to the supracausal realm, and she reached Sach Khand, the purely spiritual region at which our soul merges back in God. There, she had an experience of being with God. When she came back to physical consciousness from the experience, she said to Kabir Sahib, "Why didn't You tell me you were sitting on the throne of God?" he replied, "If I had told you before, you would not have believed it." The Sant Mat tradition is saying that the destination is also the divine Power. It is difficult to analyze at the intellectual level. God is that Power that is taking care of each of us. It is not that God really has a palace there and is sitting on a throne. The image of sitting on the throne of God is used in this anecdote as an analogy or example to help us understand the Creator. God is omnipotent, omnipresent, and not sitting on any throne. God is every place; God does not have a little small throne sitting in heaven or wherever else we may think God is. It is not like a little place in which you go to find God—God is all over—everywhere. That is difficult to understand. When Sant Darshan Singh Ji says, "You are the destination," what he is saying is that God and the Power of God flowing to us to uplift us are one and the same. At the human level, that is hard to grasp. How can God and that Power be the same? We think of the Master as the body, and we do not realize the body is not the Master. What helps us is the divine Power of God emanating from God with which we come in contact through the help of a Master. It is that Power of God which is helping us and taking us back to the Lord. Thus, it is not the physical form, but the Power working through that form that we call the Master Power.

Through certain verses and examples, saints try to clarify this to make this distinction clear to us. The tendency of some disciples, which is not correct, is to revere the body of the Master. For example, in the East, some people, out of their tradition, want to touch the feet of the Master, but they do not realize that everything we need is coming through the eyes. It is not the physical closeness of the Master; it is the spiritual closeness of the Master Power emanating from within that truly helps us, and for that, there are no barriers. For example, we think we want to find the best seat in the hall to see the Master physically sitting on a stage presenting a satsang discourse, and if some tall person is in front of us, we may get annoyed. We ask, "Why did someone give him or her a seat in the front?" However, it does not matter, because the Power penetrates through to us wherever we are. Therefore, no one is there who can stop it from getting to us. The spiritual Power, although radiating from the eyes, is actually flowing out from that form and cannot be stopped by any physical obstruction in our way. Sant Darshan Singh Ji described how when he saw Hazur Baba Sawan Singh Ji from a distance, but only saw the turban of the Master, he still would have a stirring in his being. Why? Because that Power is emanating through all parts of that physical frame, just as light shines from all parts of a light bulb. Wherever we are, that Power of God is always there to help us.

Sant Darshan Singh Ji says, "You are the destination, you are the guide and the will that impels us." Here, he is telling us that the Power of God is the will that draws us to our goal, the Power of God guides us there, and the Power of God is our destination with which we need to be one, because as we become one with that Power of God, we will be also one with God. In meditation, as we cross the inner Lights, the sky, the stars, the inner moon and the inner sun and we reach the radiant form of the Master, that radiant form becomes our inner guide. The radiant form we meet in meditation takes the appearance of the physical body and face of the Master through whom the Master Power was working when we received initiation into the Light and Sound. That becomes the radiant form for us through which Light is emitting, because we have no other means of recognizing that Power. That is the form that takes us from the physical to the astral, causal, and supracausal realms, and finally to Sach Khand, where all the coverings over our soul are removed. Sant Darshan Singh Ji says in this verse that the Power of God that flows through the Master impels or attracts our soul back to God. That Power of God that manifests as the radiant form of the Master within is the guide that takes us back to God, and that Power of God is our destination with whom we merge when we reach Sach Khand, the true Home. This is the reason why the poet is saying, "All salutations to the Lord of the Tavern!" This is why we have gratitude to the Lord of the Tavern, because it is that Master Power that helps us reach our goal of union with God.

There are numerous accounts in the lives of hundreds of thousands of disciples in which some miraculous change took place in one's condition. There are many cases of doctors perplexed to find a large tumor in someone's brain or in some other part of the body, yet it suddenly disappeared after the disciple prayed to the Master for help or talked to or wrote to him. There are also accounts of unusual reversals in many an illness. Sometimes a disciple is told that he or she has to undergo a painful operation, only to find that the situation was resolved and they only needed minor surgery or it was averted altogether. It is said that out of compassion, by taking over our karmas, a spiritual Master can reduce the pain of the gallows to a pinprick. The Master is so compassionate that the pain is often lessened to a small fraction of what it was meant to be.

In this connection, there is a beautiful account of Sant Kirpal Singh Ji in the time of Hazur Baba Sawan Singh Ji. His son, Sant Darshan Singh Ji, as a child had fallen ill and the doctors feared he may not last longer than three days. The doctors told Sant Kirpal Singh Ji to take leave from his work and sit by his bedside. Sant Kirpal Singh Ji did take leave from his office to sit with his son, but one of the days happened to be a Sunday, the day he was to conduct satsang. Sant Kirpal Singh Ji was in a dilemma: Should he listen to the doctors and sit by his child's bed on Sunday or should he do his duty to hold satsang every Sunday, as it was his responsibility to do so. Finally, Sant Kirpal Singh Ji resolved the situation by saying to himself, "To whom does this child belong? We are all in the Master's lap. We cannot control life and death; it is all in his hands. I should do the work he has given me."

Therefore, Sant Kirpal Singh Ji headed to hold satsang. After the satsang, it was noon, and Hazur resided about twenty miles away. Therefore, Sant Kirpal Singh Ji's heart said, "Why not have Hazur's darshan before going home?" Sant Kirpal Singh Ji knew the devotee's heart's desire is to have the glimpse of his Master. Therefore, he took the train to see his Master and reached there about 2 p.m. Although he had not told Hazur of his arrival, Hazur had sent a person downstairs to bring Sant Kirpal Singh Ji upstairs. Hazur was lying on his bed, and when Sant Kirpal Singh Ji entered, he sat up. Without Sant Kirpal Singh Ji telling him anything, Hazur's first words were, "What is the condition of your son?" Sant Kirpal Singh Ji informed him that the boy was seriously ill. Sant Kirpal Singh Ji then related that the doctors wanted him to stay by his bedside but he was torn between doing so and holding satsang, so he went to hold satsang. Sant Kirpal Singh Ji then further explained, "Life and death are in Master's hands." He explained that he had stopped to visit Hazur instead of returning directly home. Hazur became quiet and sat with his head in his hands looking very sorrowful. Sant Kirpal Singh Ji asked Hazur why he was in such a mood, saying, "Whoever has even a single thought of you for a moment is released of all his worries, and yet you are sitting like this, how can that be?" Hazur replied, "Well, Kirpal Singh, you have thrown all your burden on me. You have taken the load off your head, and now I must bear the burden myself!" When Sant Kirpal Singh Ji had returned home, he found that Sant Darshan Singh Ji was all right. His condition had not deteriorated as the doctors thought it would and the boy recovered. That is one example of how the Masters take the karmas on themselves and lessen our pains.

Although these seemingly miraculous things happen, they are not considered miracles. A miracle is an unexplainable happening, but what the Masters do are not considered miracles. They are merely a higher knowledge of the laws of nature that are hidden from us. A karmic debt has to be paid. Therefore, the karma is not eliminated; it is merely transferred to the Master's own body so he can pay it for us.

Today, there is a great interest in miraculous healing. Many people come and want a healing or to have the power to heal. However, the healing they are talking about is in the realm of the lower psychic powers, which in the East we call *riddhis* and *siddhis*. This is using one's power to perform a miracle. Disciples of the Masters and the Masters themselves do not engage in the use of such lower powers. The Masters want us to direct our energy into attaining the highest spiritual goal of union with God. They do not want us to waste our time and use our energy to dabble in the lower psychic powers. A story illustrates this. One day, a man was seated next to a mystic. The man performed a miracle by taking a live fish out of a tumbler of water. The mystic in response placed his hand in a burning oven and performed a miracle by bringing out a live fish. Then, the man challenged the mystic to jumping into the fire together to see who survived. The mystic finally reprimanded the man, saying, "Making miracles won't do. Let us rather drown ourselves in the ocean of nonexistence and come out wearing the garments of divine existence!" The man became silent and never tried to perform a miracle again.

Saints exhort us to use our energy to reach God, not to dabble in lower powers, miracles, and healings. When we attain higher spiritual development, these lower powers are available to us as a by-product but we are advised not to use them. Masters do not use these lower powers. The seeming miracles they perform are merely an expression of their great compassion in taking on the karmas of others. It is not done to perform miracles; it just happens spontaneously due to their love for us. It is an intervention for our behalf that spontaneously happens. The Master's heart goes out to us, and since they are in tune with the God Power, God spontaneously provides the help. The Master, having become ones with God, becomes the Beloved of God, and God accedes to his requests.

This is why the poet is praising the Lord of the Tavern. The poet realizes the amazing grace that is flowing to the disciple from the Master. It is so great that it helps us even when we are in distress. Again, this is not referring to the physical body of the Master. It refers to the Master Power that works through the human frame. That Master Power is the destination, the guide, and the will that impels us.

On our own, for lifetimes, God has not taken us back to our Eternal Home. It is by the grace of a Master who shows us the way that we return to God. He puts us in touch with the method of meditation and the contact with the Light and Sound that helps us meet God. Without this help, we may be cycling for lifetimes more without ever finding our Eternal Parent, or God. This is why Sant Darshan Singh Ji is praising the Lord of the Tavern.

THE DIVINE MIRACLE

May I behold your radiant face shorn of its veil,
May my thirsting eyes receive the wine of your
*   illumined glances,*
"Darshan" is lost in waiting for this divine miracle.
All salutations to the Lord of the tavern!
All salutations to the Lord of the tavern!
*   – Sant Darshan Singh Ji Maharaj*

To a disciple there is a yet higher miracle than the seeming one of being cured of a terrible pain. To the disciple, the Beloved unveiling himself to appear in his full radiant glory is the true miracle. This is what every disciple hopes and prays for. They know that the bliss they get from seeing the radiant form of the Master is more than any happiness that we could ever experience on earth. While a disciple may pray for help for outer problems, they know that the highest miracle is that of having the spiritual experience within, meeting the radiant form of the Master, and reuniting the soul with God.

In this verse, Sant Darshan Singh Ji uses an example prevalent in the times in which he grew up. In some traditions, the women wore a veil to cover their face and that was only to be removed by the husband in the privacy of their chambers. They considered it a sacrilege if anyone else sees the woman behind the veil. It was common in India in the past. He is taking this as another example for us to understand the Master Power. When he says, "May I behold your radiant face shorn of its veil," he is painting an image that there is a veil in front of the Master. What is that veil? He is using the veil as another poetic analogy for the body of the Master acting as a veil to cover the spiritual Power working within and through that physical form. He explains that when we look at the physical body of a Master, we do not see the Master Power as that is spirit. In the verse, he says, "Let me see you as you truly are." Let me experience you as the Power, not as the body, because I can see the body, but it is only a veil covering the true spiritual essence and Power. The true Master is not the body, but the Power or Master Power that works through the body. He requests humbly, "Please be gracious to me and let me see you in your true glory." Just like in the historical anecdote when Indu Mati saw Kabir Sahib in his full glory within, she realized who the Master really was—not the body, but the spiritual Power behind or working through the body, similarly, that request is being made in this verse. He says that your face is heavenly, but you have a veil in front of your face and all I see is your physical face. Sant Darshan Singh Ji in this verse is requesting the Master to please remove this veil so he can see his spiritual essence, his radiant form within, and ultimately as he traverses to the highest spiritual realm to experience him in his true essence—the formless state where we experience reality as it really is.

Sant Darshan Singh Ji's poetry is so rich that one image or word can have multiple meanings. Another analogy of veil being referred to in this verse is the veil of darkness we first see when we close our eyes in meditation. The poet is asking the

Beloved to remove the veil to reveal the inner radiant form of the Master in its true glory. We can see the outer form of the Master with our physical eyes. We can experience the peace, bliss, and upliftment from the physical presence of the Master. However, the radiant form is even more bliss-giving, ecstasy-producing, and intoxicating than what we experience from the outer form. The radiant form is the form that the divine Power takes so we can recognize it and go with it on our inner journey. At our level of understanding, we recognize a face with a human form. Until we can see with our inner eyes and hear with our inner ears, we have not yet reached the level of being able to identify with spirit. That is why the Master Power takes on a form that we can recognize. We then know it is the Master guiding us. Yet, when we reach the highest stages, form merges into formlessness. In the higher regions, God is formless. We at our intellectual level cannot understand that. At the lower levels, we recognize the outer form of the Master physically, and the radiant form that has the features, but is more radiant and ethereal, illumined by Light. As we journey with that form, we ultimately reach a stage in which that form merges with the formless and is all Light.

In the next line of verse, Sant Darshan Singh Ji says, "May my thirsting eyes receive the wine of your illumined glances." He is describing the thirst we need to have in our soul.

In this connection, there is a story about a young man who wanted to see his Master in meditation. He was trying to meditate to reach the radiant form within, but was not getting there. No matter how hard he tried, he could not experience it. He sought help. He found someone who had been meditating successfully for a long time. He asked him, "I have been meditating, but I am not seeing the radiant form of the Master within. What should

I do?" He received advice in the form of an unusual suggestion, saying, "I want you to try something. On Friday night, eat food with a lot of salt in it, and after eating that do not drink any water. Do your meditation, and then go to sleep. Try that and see what happens to you."

The young man thought, "This is an unusual request. He is telling me to eat more salt. Well, he has been meditating for a long time successfully, so he must know what he is talking about."

On Friday night, the young man ate heavily-salted food, but did not drink any water. He meditated and when finished went to sleep. All night long, he dreamt about water, as he was extremely thirsty.

When he awoke he returned to his advisor and said, "I did what you asked, but I did not see the Master within. Because I was so thirsty, all night long I was thinking about water and dreaming of drinking water. I am so thirsty, I feel like I am on fire!"

His advisor said, "Eating salty food gave you so much thirst that the entire night you dreamt of nothing but water. If you were to have such a thirst for finding the Master within with this much intensity all the time as you thought about the water all night long, you would definitely have the blessing of reaching the radiant form of the Master within."

This account describes the kind of passion and zeal we need to find God. Meditation is not just a mechanical act. The fire of desire for God must light our meditation so that the flames of our soul can rise to the heavens.

Sant Darshan Singh Ji says in the verse that this thirst in my eyes, meaning the thirst in my soul, needs to be quenched.

He says, "I am thirsty to know you. I am thirsty to be with you. I am thirsting so I can be totally satiated. May my thirsting eyes receive the wine of your illumined glances." The words are beautiful. He is addressing his prayer to his Master, because he recognizes that the glances of the Master are such that they intoxicate us and uplift us within so that we can take the inner journey back to God. This is why he uses the term, "the wine of your illumined glances," because those glances are illumined with Light that will uplift the soul back to God. He says that since the Master has achieved oneness with God, his eyes are thirsting for the intoxication that comes through him so he too can attain oneness with the Lord.

Often, Sant Darshan Singh Ji described beautifully that that grace comes from the eyes of the Master to the eyes of the disciple, from the heart of the Master to the heart of the disciple, and from the soul of the Master to the soul of the disciple. He wants such a glance that puts one in such intoxication that we transcend our physical consciousness to reach spiritual consciousness and take the inner journey back to union with God. He prays for this divine connection, a bond that is lasting. He says that everything else except such a glance is transitory, like coming and going, or ships passing in the night. That is why he says that my eyes are thirsting, so please pour out the divine Wine coming from your illumined eyes. Sant Kirpal Singh Ji used to say that two-thirds of spirituality come from the eyes of the Master. It is only one-third of spirituality that comes through word of mouth as in the books, readings, and outer spoken words to which we listen at satang. For this reason, emphasis is placed in Sant Mat on being in the presence of the Master. It is being in that presence that we not only hear the words, but that the spiritual radiation washes away layers of mind, matter, and illusion that have been covering our soul for lifetimes. That is why we may have witnessed hundreds of thousands of people in our lifetime flocking to be with these great spiritual Masters so they could get a glimpse of them and be in that state where the obstructive layers surrounding their soul could be peeled off. Sant Darshan Singh Ji says in this verse, "I am thirsting to know God, so please shower your spiritual energy on me so that my thirst can be quenched."

In the next line of verse, he says, "Darshan is lost waiting for this divine miracle." A true devotee only wants the darshan or glance of the Master, both outside in which we see him physically and inside in which we see his radiant form. We want to reach the radiant form of the Master within in meditation, because that form is our guide who will take our soul to attain merger in God. That is what a true disciple wants. That experience propels us to our goal of oneness with God.

Difficulties are a part of life. Sometimes our business is not running well, finances are going kaput, or we have physical ailments or relationships that do not work as we would like them to work. Those problems are all part of life. People who only focus on those problems have a harder time reaching their goal of finding God because it distracts them from going within and meditating with full concentration and accuracy. Those disciples who instead focus on meditation instead of their outer problems recognize that they are using their time more beneficially as that will lead them to the radiant form of the Master within. Such disciples realize that if we put in our time, focus, and attention to reach that radiant form, that form will guide us through the inner spiritual realms until our soul merges back in God.

When we attend a spiritual or holiday retreat program or a satsang, may the love and the Light of the Master Power flowing out to us uplift us from the physical to the Divine. Through initiation into the inner Light and Sound and daily meditation, we can definitely attain our spiritual goal of union with God. By focusing our attention in the spiritual arena, finding time for meditation daily, and putting in the effort, grace will come. Sant Darshan Singh Ji would say that this is a path of grace and effort. It is God's grace that we are on the path. Then, when we put in a little effort by meditating, by keeping an introspection diary of our daily thoughts, words, and deeds to improve in our ethical living, by doing selfless service, and by attending satsang, we receive more grace. When we get more grace, we are happy and want to put in more effort. When we put in more effort, we receive more grace, and the arcs of effort and grace will complete the circle when we reach our goal. It is through grace of God and the great Masters that as we pass through this life, our attention is focused on the Divine. With their guidance we can all reach our goal in this lifetime.

Once we have a taste of the intoxication from the Master's eyes, whether being with the Master at a holiday spiritual gathering, a satsang, or any gathering at which he is present, we know that his glance brings more fulfillment than any joy of this world. We want that bliss again and again. It becomes our continuous longing and desire. We know that the bliss of the outer darshan is but a reflection of the greater bliss awaiting us within. That is why the disciple prays to have the inner darshan of the Master's radiant form.

We can enjoy this radiant form by meditating. We must sit with accuracy and full concentration, gazing into the middle of what lies in front of us. While doing so, we can keep thoughts from distracting us if we mentally repeat the five Charged Words given by the Master at the time of initiation into the Light and Sound. While meditating in this manner, we will see Light within. We may see Light of any color. Then, by looking into the middle of what comes before us, inner vistas of sky, stars, moon, and sun will open up for us. By continuing to look into the middle of what we see, ultimately we find the radiant form of the Master. We then go with the radiant form, which takes us on an inner journey through the astral region, the causal region, and supracausal region, until we reach our eternal Home, the lap of God.

Those who have not received initiation can try the introductory form called *Jyoti* Meditation and mentally repeat any Name of God with which they feel comfortable to get a taste of the peace and happiness within.

Although the disciple may pray for more grace, prayer without effort is not enough; he or she must also do the inner work of sitting regularly in meditation. It is a matter of effort and grace. We make the effort by sitting for two and a half hours daily in accurate, regular meditation. We must have a ruling passion to meet God. The increased grace then comes, giving us our souls' desire to see the radiant form of the Master to take us back to God.

It is also not enough to merely pray for union with God without doing the spiritual practice of sitting in meditation. We must sit in meditation for the prescribed time with zeal and passion. Then, increased grace can come. Our prayers can then be answered by the combination of effort and grace, and we will be blessed with the divine illuminating form of the Master.

Then, our inner spiritual journey can begin.

If we are lucky enough to experience the grace of the Master that manifests in many ways, such as by having our distress relieved or by finding the radiant form of the Master, we will understand the great praise for the Master in this verse. We too will be expressing our gratitude to the Master, as Sant Darshan Singh Ji does, by also proclaiming:

All salutations to the Lord of the Tavern!
All salutations to the Lord of the Tavern!

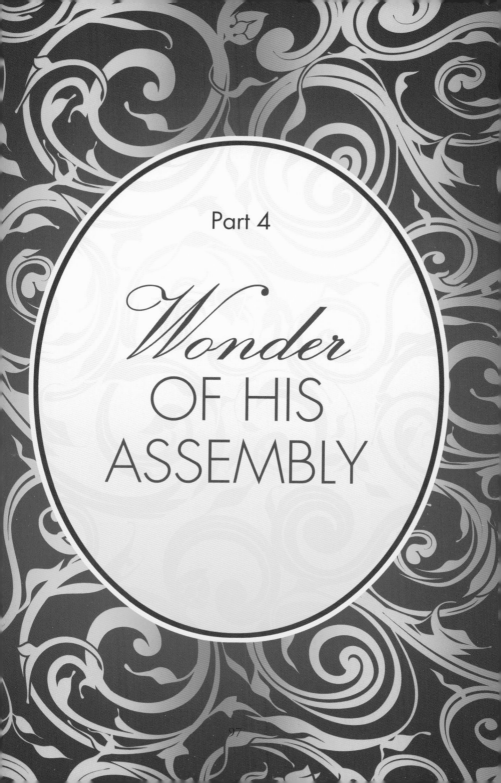

Part 4

Wonder
OF HIS
ASSEMBLY

Part 4

Wonder
OF HIS ASSEMBLY

DANCING IN ECSTACY

How to describe the wonder of his assembly?
Both the goblet and the flask are dancing in ecstasy.
– Sant Darshan Singh Ji Maharaj

Sant Darshan Singh Ji describes the benevolence of the spiritual Master, the gains we derive from his company, and what we receive in his assembly. He gives us a glimpse of what a disciple experiences in the spiritual gathering. Anyone seeking the Lord is invited. It is not limited to those from one country or creed. It is an assembly of seekers after truth and lovers of God.

In the verse, he asks how we can describe the wonders of his assembly. What is unique and wondrous about this gathering? Sant Darshan Singh Ji's poetry draws on mystic imagery. When trying to express spiritual truths, people can relate to imagery from their everyday life. In this verse, he elaborates further on the image of a tavern where people go to drink wine or liquor to be intoxicated as a way to escape their troubles. After drinking, though, they suffer many side effects such as having a hangover. In this example, there is a bartender and an assembly. In a bar, all kinds of people gather. They do not ask other people from which faith or country they come. They simply sit down together and drink because they are all trying to be intoxicated. They do not think about the difficulties that they may undergo from the effects of their drinking. Sant Darshan Singh Ji uses that example of the tavern to describe the spiritual assembly of seekers and lovers of the Creator.

In a previous verse, we explored how in mysticism, the tavern is used as an image referring to the assembly in which one is in the presence of a spiritual Master. The Master is the Cupbearer who serves the divine Wine or the holy Word or Naam, the Light and Sound of God, two primary manifestations of God into expression. In this verse, he introduces the image of the goblet and the flask. These refer respectively to the Master and the disciple. The Master is the one from whom the divine Wine is poured and the disciple is the flask into whom that Godly Wine is poured.

When we think of the word "Cupbearer," we think of one who serves drinks to others in a tavern. Ironically, the bartender remains sober, but serves alcoholic drinks that people order to become intoxicated or drunk. If the bartender is not sober, then he or she cannot do the job of doling out drinks to others. That person needs to be in his or her senses. When Sant Darshan Singh Ji describes the state of the physical bartender, he refers to one being in one's physical senses. Yet, in this verse, he says that everyone in this assembly is in ecstasy. They are all dancing. When the image of dancing is used, it describes a state in which people are joyous. When he says that both the goblet and the flask are dancing in ecstasy he is describing how all the people in that assembly are filled with happiness. They are all in ecstasy because they are receiving the intoxicating divine Wine through the eyes of the Cupbearer, or the Master. The divine Wine is a poetic analogy for the spiritual Power of God flowing through the physical form of the Master. Being one with the divine Power, the Master is in ecstasy himself. Since God, the Source from which the divine Wine is coming, is in ecstasy, then the state of the whole assembly that drinks from that is also becoming more ecstatic and blissful.

In this world, as people experience difficulties, they may feel disenchanted and think that drinking liquor is going to solve their problems. They do not realize that after being intoxicated for several hours, they will have to undergo difficulties that arise in their lives from drinking. On the spiritual path, as part of the requirements for initiation into the Light and Sound, one must give up alcoholic drinks and drugs that are intoxicating and hallucinogenic. Why? We are trying to meditate to raise our consciousness to go back to God. Because drinking alcohol and taking hallucinogenic drugs lowers our consciousness, we are asked to avoid them. We want to raise our consciousness, not lower it.

In this connection, there is a story from history about a king who had a son. The king wanted his son, the prince, to grow up and experience life as a commoner so he could understand the difficulties of the people. Thus, he did not lavish on him anything that would spoil or pamper him. Instead, he treated his son as an ordinary boy. The prince gained experience in doing trades like other people. This often involved tasks such as working with his hands. He ate plain food, slept on a hard bed, and sometimes suffered hunger and cold, as did the common people of his times. This toughened him up and also filled him with compassion for the plight of others.

When the boy was twelve, he took a trip with his mother, the queen, to visit his grandfather who was also a king, but in another nation. His grandfather was a rich and powerful monarch with a large kingdom.

When his grandfather saw his grandson, he was impressed with how handsome, tall, and strong he was. He told the boy's mother he wanted the boy to stay and live with him in his kingdom. The grandfather gave the boy many gifts to make him happy.

While the boy was staying with him, the king wanted to have a feast for his grandson. The king had the most elaborate food prepared and laid it out on the serving tables. He arranged for music and dancing. He told the prince to invite as many friends as he wanted to the feast.

When the day of the feast arrived, everything was set up with much pomp and show, with servants lined up in their serving outfits. Musicians and dancers took their place. Yet, in the banquet hall only two people arrived—the king's daughter and his grandson. Not a single other guest came.

The king asked the boy, "How is it that no one is arriving? I told you that you could invite as many friends as you wanted. The feast is prepared, but no one is showing up to partake of it. Where are your friends?"

The prince replied, "I did not invite anyone."

The king asked, "Why?"

The prince answered, "Where I come from, we do not have such feasts. If someone is hungry, he eats some bread and a regular meal. We never make such elaborate feasts with expensive food. We all just eat regular meals and share what we have."

His grandfather, the king, did not know if he should be angry with the boy or proud of him, so he did not respond. The king merely said, "Well, now that this food is prepared what do you propose we do with it? The feast was for you, so it is your food now. Do what you want with it."

The prince said, "I can divide it up and distribute it then." He thought of all the people who had helped him in life and gave them each a portion of the food. He gave some food to the king's officer who taught him how to ride a horse. He gave some to an elderly servant who took care of his grandfather. He then gave the rest to the young serving women who took care of his mother. The rest he had distributed to the commoners in the kingdom.

One of the king's servants, his cupbearer, was disappointed and upset that the boy did not give him a portion of the feast. The king also noticed that his cupbearer was left out. Since the cupbearer was his favorite servant, the king also felt slighted by the boy's action of not giving him any portion of food from the feast.

The king asked the prince, "Why didn't you give any food to my cupbearer?"

The prince replied, "I do not think he is doing a good job for you. I do not really like the way he acts. He acts proud and overbearing. He thinks too much of himself, especially when he waits on you."

The king said, "Well, he should think much of himself, after all, he is a skilled and able cupbearer."

The prince said, "Maybe he is, but if you make me your

cupbearer, I will do a better job than he does."

The king was impressed with his grandson's willful nature and assertiveness. He thought he should let the boy have a try at being his cupbearer to see how he does. He told his grandson to come the next morning and he would try him out to see if he would make a good cupbearer.

The next day, the grandson came dressed up like a cupbearer, wearing the proper uniform and carrying himself with grace and dignity. On his arm was draped a white napkin. In his hand was a cup of wine that he held with the proper etiquette.

The king asked him for a glass of wine. The boy handed the wine to the king.

The mother and king applauded the boy for the perfect etiquette and grace he showed when serving.

The king said, "You did very well, except you forgot one thing."

"What is that?" asked the prince.

The king said, "Normally, before serving the king, the cupbearer pours a bit of wine first and tastes it before handing the cup to me to make sure it is of good quality. You forgot to do this."

The prince said, "I did not forget to do that at all."

The prince's mother asked, "Then, why did you not do it?"

The prince said, "I did not taste it first because I thought there was poison in the wine."

The king was shocked and yelled out, "Poison?"

The prince said, "Yes, this is poison. I am not going to drink it. I saw that the other day when you had dinner with your ministers, I noticed that the wine that was served to you made you act strangely. I noted that after the guests drank the wine, they kept on drinking until they began to be rowdy and talk and act foolishly. They were singing loudly, walking crookedly, and saying inappropriate things. The atmosphere became bad. Even you, my dear grandfather, acted in the same rowdy way. You acted as if you had forgotten you had the dignity of a king. You started dancing in a funny way and then fell flat on the floor. You lay unconscious and then got sick to your stomach when you woke up. It was so undignified. I am afraid even to take a sip of anything that causes people to act that way. Thus, I consider wine a poison."

The king asked if the boy's father, the king, ever drank wine.

The boy said, "He does not drink to get intoxicated and drunk. He drinks only those things such as non-alcoholic drinks to quench his thirst. That is why I will not partake of wine, even if I am a cupbearer."

This story from history illustrates the attitude that those on the spiritual path have toward alcohol. They know that although other people drink to get intoxicated to forget their difficulties for a while, it also lowers one's consciousness, causing one to lose awareness of the physical senses and behave in ways harmful to oneself and others. They see how shy people who may have difficulty approaching others to socialize feel if they have a drink or two. They would lose their inhibitions so they could talk to others. They then may feel, "Because I am no longer in my physical senses from drinking, I have an excuse to do whatever I want." Little do they realize the difficulties drinking brings into their lives. It negatively affects people physically, intellectually, emotionally, financially, and spiritually.

For this reason, at the time of initiation into the path of Sant Mat, seekers give up liquor and intoxicating, hallucinogenic drugs.

Why? Liquor and intoxicating drugs destroy our consciousness, making us less conscious. They defile our true state, putting us in an unconscious rather than in a more conscious state. Taking initiation is a step towards becoming more conscious of who we are and of what the reality of life is.

The boy had principles and lived up to them, even under pressure from others to act differently. Some noble characteristics needed on the spiritual way are to stick to our commitment to be teetotalers and avoid drugs and alcohol that cause us to be intoxicated.

Instead, we get our intoxication from the spiritual Cupbearer who serves the divine Wine of Naam, the Light and Sound of God. The goblet and the flask dance in ecstasy because they are becoming more conscious of their closeness to the Lord. This divine Wine or the Power of God gives an intoxication that is spiritual and does not lower our consciousness. It uplifts us into the Light and Sound current, upon which our soul can journey through the higher realms back to God. There is nothing better than that. What else can compare to realizing that we are a part of the Creator of everything? In this verse, the soul is dancing in ecstasy because it is experiencing an intoxication that leads us to merge into the eternal bliss of God.

Unfortunately, because the soul encased in the human body is suppressed by the wiles of the mind, we are not aware of this ecstasy. As we pass through our day-to-day existence, we are missing the opportunity to know ourselves as soul. Our mind creates desires within us that distract our attention from the treasures within and pulls it into the outer world. Due to these attractions to the world, the time we have is wasted and passes away. Saints exhort us to focus on the Divine. When our soul is connected with the Source of all energy, the divine Light and Sound of God, it soars into the inner spiritual regions.

How can we reach that state? Sant Darshan Singh Ji through this verse tells us that we can reach states of ecstasy when we come into the assembly of a divine Cupbearer. The dancing in this verse is not referring to physical dancing where everyone gets up and starts moving their body to the music; rather, it refers to the soul that is dancing within themselves. Although the soul is contained within the physical body, it can have experiences that transcend physical body-consciousness. Some people may refer to this as "out of the body experiences" but they are actually not "out of the body experiences"; rather, they are experiences of the Beyond that take places while our body may be sitting in a physical location, such as in an assembly or the satsang arena. Many times, people who are receptive as they sit in a satsang may become oblivious to their physical surroundings. They are so receptive that the love of the Lord and spiritual radiation coming to us through the Master Power reaches the depths of the soul, causing the soul to soar into regions Beyond. It is a question of how receptive we are. The Power of God is always coming in our direction. Those who are receptive gain from that Power and can be uplifted into the regions Beyond. Those who still think about other things while sitting in satsang or whose attention cannot be totally focused on God, the spiritual radiation still comes to them, but it is deflected because we are not open to receive it. We then do not gain from it as much as we could have.

If we are receptive, we receive everything coming in our direction. As it reaches the depths of our soul, then the soul can lift off. If we are not receptive, blockages come from our mind to stop us from receiving all that is coming to us. The mind wants us to be involved with only the activities of the world. It will do its best so we do not reach our goals. Sant Darshan Singh Ji through his verses is not only telling us what the assembly is like, but is also guiding us to the state of merger with God. As souls, we all have a part of God within. God is not somewhere else in the sky or clouds. We can experience God as a part of us. That experience comes when we sit in silence. In the stillness of the body, the soul is dancing. That is why as we sit in silence and soar into inner regions we experience stillness associated with states of bliss. It is hard to understand this when we look at the outer world, because when we are joyous we feel this needs to be expressed through physical activity like dancing for joy. However, in the spiritual arena, we meditate for the soul to experience well-being and joyfulness of being uplifted within. That state is not limited to only a few. Sant Kirpal Singh Ji said that what one person can do, so can another. It is a question of focusing our attention in the spiritual arena.

In the assembly, everyone is in ecstasy. The Master Power, which gives us a spiritual boost by connecting us to the Creator and focusing our attention on the Divine, is also in ecstasy The role of the Master Power is to take souls back to God. As souls are uplifted back to God, the Master Power is in ecstasy, too, because it is fulfilling its job of guiding souls back to the Lord and taking them off the wheel of transmigration. That gives happiness to the Master Power. Even in this world, a teacher is happy when the student does well. As we meditate and travel on the spiritual journey, that gives happiness to the Master Power. This is why the goblet and the flask referred to in this verse are dancing in ecstasy. The ones drinking are in ecstasy, and the

Master Power is in ecstasy.

Here, in this verse, Sant Darshan Singh Ji is not saying the outer Master is in ecstasy, but the power of God, the Master Power, is in ecstasy. It is that Master Power that initiates us, it is the Master Power that guides us, and it is the Master Power that has the responsibility to take our souls back to God. It is the Master Power that is in ecstasy when disciples gather together in the satsang as that is radiating to every soul to guide them towards the goal of union with God.

Every time we read these verses, we need to think deeply about what they mean. Sometimes when we read a translation, we may only receive half or less of what is really written there. The depths of the meaning of the words are so great that it is difficult to understand them in another language. Sometimes there are not even the words in another language to describe a verse. For centuries, satsangs given by Masters have generally been based on the writings or verses of previous Masters as they try to explain their deeper meanings. Whenever saints came, what they spoke and wrote was absolute Truth. The Truth they spoke in the year 5,000 B.C or 1 B.C. is the same as today. They are all giving out the Truth, although they may have been spoken in different languages or in terminology used at the time they lived which may no longer be popular or in use today. Sometimes a clear understanding of the terms may be lost as they were translated into other languages, or when the language and terms of the times changed even within the same language. For this reason, we are lucky to be living in an age with a wealth of communication media. There are photographs of Hazur Baba Sawan Singh Ji. We have some sound recordings of Sant Kirpal Singh Ji. We have many movies with sound and videos of Sant Kirpal Singh Ji and Sant Darshan Singh Ji. The technology is such that we can see and hear what they were saying coming right from their own lips, and which do not need any interpretation. Yet, in the old times, technology was not there. Therefore, to understand the spiritual path better, one always needed interpretation of writings given in languages of the past in which different terminology was used. As we go forward, there is much more material available to us in different media in the satsang that we can make use of to understand the spiritual path.

We should consider the question, "Why do we come to the satsang?" Is it to socialize, or show people we are spiritual because we went to a meditation program? Or do we come to gain spiritual benefit? To be in a spiritual gathering should mean that we want to grow spiritually and know God. The gain we seek at satsang is for our soul.

Sant Kirpal Singh Ji gave this example, saying: "If I were sitting in a room, and outside the door there was a small chamber with a lawyer sitting there, and in front of that area was another room with a banker sitting there, and in front of that room was another with a doctor sitting there, most people would never make it to the room where I was. Most people would first go to the room with the doctor because many people who come to the great saints first want their physical ailments removed. Whether they are sick themselves or have a physical problem, or their parents, cousins, uncles, or aunts, brothers or sisters, or someone they know is sick, they want to be cured. I think that most of the people who come want to be physically relieved of their pain. That is why in this example he put the doctor in the front room. They see the doctor and after their illness is gone, they too are gone. A few people come because they have monetary problems. Their jobs or businesses are not doing well or the world economy has gone bad. They try to see the banker, get some money, and are satisfied with that, so, they are gone. They never go further to see the Master in the inner room. A few other people come who have litigations going on. They have legal problems. If the lawyer solves their problem, very few would go further to reach the room where the Master is sitting. Sant Kirpal Singh Ji would say, "Very few people would come to see me." They would stop at the room of the doctor, banker, and lawyer. He is saying that few people come to the Master for spirituality; most come to have their problems taken care of, either physically, financially, or legally. If we gain in those three areas, we are only gaining at the physical level. However, we can gain much more from the Master by receiving spiritual upliftment. He can take us out of the wheel of transmigration. The guidance of the Master can help our soul reach Sach Khand. That is what we should seek.

There are many examples of the saints making comments to disciples saying, "If you would have asked me for any boon at a time when I was with the Lord, you could have received anything for which you asked; instead, you only asked for something of the world, and that is why you received only that. If you had asked for God, you would have gotten God." We need to be careful as to what we ask for, and if we only stick to things of the physical, emotional, or intellectual level, then that is what we receive. A true prayer should be for spiritual upliftment so we can be guided towards our goal of reaching union with God and being off the wheel of transmigration.

When we come to satsang, we should leave all our other thoughts outside the hall. If we are there and only thinking about other things of the world, we are not gaining because we are not receptive at that time. Our attention is only focusing on the outer world. An empty cup is one that receives. To be an empty cup means being in a state of humility. If we are filled with ego, we cannot receive anything. The saints say that to receive something, the tap needs to be above and the cup needs to be below. The water flows from the tap to the cup. The cup needs to be empty and held below the tap. That is what humility is. Being receptive and living with the principle of "sweet is Thy will" are states in which we need to be to gain truly from a spiritual Master. Our ego keeps us from gaining spiritually. Our ego wants us to be a certain way and comes between our soul and God. Those who control their egos are well equipped to have their soul merge back in God.

Whenever we have an opportunity to be in the presence of a true Cupbearer, then we should be ready to drink the intoxicating Nectar and let its bubbling Wine fill our cups.

THE RADIANCE OF THE FRIEND

One cannot see the Lord with these outer eyes;
Only with the inner eye can one see the radiance
  of the Friend
            – Sant Darshan Singh Ji Maharaj

This verse of a ghazal of Sant Darshan Singh Ji describes the difference between the outer eyes and the inner eyes. Here, the Master Power is being called our Friend. Sant Darshan Singh Ji has used this term "Friend" in another verse that says:

I have no Friend except my Beloved,
I have no work except his love.

We need to realize that the Master Power is our one and only true Friend in this life. No one else in life can give us what we can get from the Master Power. Why? Every relationship in this world is limited. Some who are near and dear to us may physically pass away before we do, or those relationships we may think were close may end in a separation due to a misunderstanding. Any relationship could have difficulties. However, the Master Power is always there for us. It is not judging us. In any relationship someone is thinking, "I am doing this for that person, but what is he or she doing for me?" However, with the Master Power, it is a one-way street—love simply flows to us because the Master Power does not need anything from us. The Master Power knows only to give, give, and give.

What does he give? From the Master Power, we get a firsthand inner experience that leads to the reunion of our soul with God. Spoken words can only penetrate the intellect, but the spiritual radiation that penetrates the depths of our soul truly transforms us. Transformation comes when we experience the inner Light and Sound. We need to cross the threshold into the Divine. That is the reason that in Sant Mat, emphasis is placed on meditating so we can have that transcendent revelation for ourselves.

This verse says that one cannot see God with these outer eyes. Why? God is spirit and consciousness and not defined by or limited to a physical form. The physical eyes, only capable of seeing the physical world, are not capable of seeing spiritual Light. To know God, we need to rise into a spiritual state.

This verse is also telling us that with our outer eyes we cannot really recognize or see the true Master. With the physical eyes, we can only see the outer or physical form of the Master, and nothing beyond that. However, that is not what the Master truly is. The true Master is the Master Power. It is only with our inner or spiritual eye that we can see the radiance of the Friend, which in this verse refers to the radiant form of the Master.

Our outer eyes are made to see objects only of this physical world. Our physical eyes are capable of receiving a small range of light waves in this physical universe. In fact, our eyes cannot penetrate through the skin of a physical body to see the bones or organs within it without the aid of X-rays and MRIs. We only know what is within the body through instrumentation. We also cannot hear beyond certain frequencies. Humans cannot hear above or below a certain range, while other animals can hear higher and lower frequencies. We are limited as to what we can see and hear through our physical eyes and ears.

However, as we transcend physical consciousness and reach our true state, at the level of the soul, then we are able to see the Friend, the radiant Friend, which is the radiant form of the Master.

Sant Darshan Singh Ji is telling us that we need to transcend physical consciousness to experience the Divine. Then, what the Master truly is will be revealed to us. By reaching that stage, we really experience the Master.

When someone asked Sant Kirpal Singh Ji in the early days of his discipleship how great was his Master, Hazur Baba Sawan Singh Ji, he said, "I do not know how great he is, but I know that he is surely far, far above me—far above that which I wanted." To understand this, we can take the example of a student going to a kindergarten teacher, who teaches him or her how to read and write the letters of the alphabet, the ABCs, and subjects like that. If years later, that same student grows older, goes to middle school, and happens to have the same teacher, the teacher is now teaching him or her how to read higher-level books and to write essays. Suppose that teacher is also trained to teach high school, the student who goes to him or her will learn higher-level subjects such as literature, calculus, or chemistry. Then, if that student had that same teacher in college, he or she would be learning the intricacies of the various subjects. Then, if that student went for a Master's degree or Ph.D., that teacher could help guide him or her further in those higher-level subject areas. When one first goes to the teacher in the kindergarten to learn from him or her, one does not know the depth of the teacher's knowledge. At that stage, the teacher will only teach you to the level of kindergarten skills. In fact, there are teachers who are only trained to teach at a kindergarten level. Each successive year, one needs to go to another teacher who can teach at a higher grade level. If one goes to middle school, one needs someone who can teach at that level. If one goes to high school or college, someone else is required who can teach up to those levels. The middle school teacher may only know enough to teach middle school subjects but does not know enough to teach at the high school level. The high school teacher may not know enough to teach at the college level. The college instructor may not know enough to teach at the graduate school level. The teacher can only teach at the level in which he or she knows and for which he or she is qualified. As we advance, we know more and more of what capabilities a teacher has.

The same holds true for a spiritual teacher. If a Master has only gone to the first level on the spiritual journey, that is where he can take you. If the Master has gone to the second level, maybe he can take you to the second level. If the Master has gone to the third level, maybe he can take you to the third level. If one finds a spiritual Master who has gone to the highest spiritual realm and reunited his soul with God, he also can take you beyond the physical level to the highest spiritual level to reach union with God. To get off the wheel of transmigration, our soul needs to merge back in God at the highest spiritual level, Sach Khand.

It is said that we can only know a Master to the extent to which he reveals himself. At first, we may see the Master only as an outer, physical form. Until our inner eye is opened, we mostly take the Master as an outer teacher who gives talks and outer guidance. This is one of the reasons that when a Master is asked what to call him, he may respond as did Hazur Baba Sawan Singh Ji, Sant Kirpal Singh Ji, or Sant Darshan Singh Ji when they said, "Take me as a friend, or an elder brother. Then, when you go inside, you can call me anything you like." As we progress spiritually, we find the Master's help at higher and higher levels and come to appreciate more and more of his divine greatness.

When the attention of the Master falls on us, our inner eye is opened, which is what happens at the time of the holy initiation. What is initiation? Initiation is partaking of some consciousness of the Master Power. We need that Power to open the inner eye. When our inner eye is opened through the Master's attention, we recognize his ability to put us in touch with the inner Light and Sound of God. As that doorway opens, we are equipped to travel to the inner spiritual regions Beyond. Along with opening the single or third eye to see and hear the Light and Sound and inner vistas within, when we invert our attention in meditation, we find that radiant form of the Master to guide us further on our spiritual journey. The ways within are intricate. The radiant form guides us so we are not waylaid or distracted as we travel to reach our goal of union with God in Sach Khand.

Initiation is a spiritual birth, in which we are born into our spiritual life. That is when our journey starts. Sant Darshan Singh Ji says that if we want to meet God, our voyage begins when our inner eye is opened. When we have that spiritual boost, we realize that he is more than just the physical body. We truly see the Friend in meditation, when we see the radiant or etheric form who serves as our guide. As we progress in our meditations and proceed higher through the astral and causal realms, we see more of the glory of the Friend. The higher we go within, the more we recognize the greatness of the Master. As we reach the highest level, we discover the Master to be Satguru, or one who is merged in the Lord. We find the Master is one with the Divine Power that is all consciousness.

Thus, on the outer level to begin with, we only see a physical being; it is only with the spiritual eye that we can experience the Master Power. The Masters exhort us to do our own meditation practices and lead a spiritual life so that we can attain what they have reached. Then, with our own inner eye, we can see for ourselves the radiance of our Friend.

If we wish to uncover the mysteries of the Master and find out who he really is, then we need to devote more time to our spiritual practices. We should not become complacent. The firsthand experience is needed. The outer form of the Master and its spiritual radiation is a help but not the end goal. We should use that as a boost to help us be propelled within. There is no substitute for daily, accurate meditations. Let us commit to going within to see the radiance of the Friend and to meet God.

Part 5

Spiritually
DELVE

Part 5

Spiritually Delve

Spiritually delve
To be fully alive.
Don't stay on the side.
You need to dive.
With diving you rise.
What a sweet surprise.
— Sant Rajinder Singh Ji Maharaj

Every New Year, people generally make resolutions. They evaluate what happened in the last year to decide in what areas they want to improve, what they want to keep, and what they want to discard because it brought pain into their lives. As we start each New Year, it is important to ask ourselves in what direction we want to go.

New Year's is a time to ring out the old and bring in the new. Each year, we have a birthday, which can be considered the first day of the next year of our life. New Year's is like a communal birthday for the world, in which we collectively celebrate the start of the next year. It is a time in which we can begin anew, renew our dreams, and put them into action. Some people take their birthday as a time to throw out old habits and start afresh. New Year's is an opportunity for all of us on the same day to do the same thing—bring in the new to our lives.

In this connection, there is an account of a woman whose job changed, requiring her to move. The woman hired professional packers and movers to help her. Generally, when we move, we take things to our new home that are useful to us and throw out what is useless. It is a weeding out process for deciding what to keep and what to toss. The packers asked the woman what to move and what to leave behind or throw out. Unfortunately, she was so busy and in such a rush that she had no time to weed out anything. She then said, "I have no time—just bring everything." She then left for work and they continued packing up her house. When moving day came, they moved all her things in. When they left and she began to settle in and unpack, she was shocked at what she saw. The first box she opened had garbage in it. There was old junk and bags of garbage from her trash bins. She opened up a second box and it also was filled with trash.

She immediately called up the moving company and complained, saying, "What have you done? There is garbage in the boxes. Why did you move trash and garbage into my new house?"

They simply said, "We asked you what you wanted to move, and you told us to move everything, so that is what we did."

Similarly, as we move from one year to a new year, we have to take some time to decide what to keep. We cannot say that we are so busy that we do not know, so let us take all the garbage with us. It is better that we discard the garbage that is not good in our lives, such as areas in which we have shortcomings or in which we are not doing well. Those areas we should discard. Each year, we have an opportunity to throw out the old and bring in the new. It is a weeding out process in which we need to evaluate what habits we want to keep and which ones we want to eliminate.

Cleaning our house helps us screen out those things that do not benefit us. We can choose to lead our lives so that everything we do is useful to us. If we are carrying a lot of baggage with us, or spending time in a direction in which we are not gaining, we may not be living in a way that fulfills our life's purpose. This results in a struggle within us in which the mind drags us into the world and the soul wants to go back to God.

In this connection, there is a story about a family that moved from one village to another. The family included a young daughter who was at a marriageable age. The girl had finished her studies, had taken work as a house cleaner, and was doing a good job cleaning people's houses.

The family started looking for a suitable husband for their daughter. They sought out all the eligible bachelors in the village and interviewed them to see who would be best suited to marry her. They found a fine young man who had set up a business for himself as a coal burner, burning charcoal for a living. The charcoal was used to create fire to warm the homes of the people in his community. The parents thought this job was a stable one in which he made a steady income. He also was a kind fellow, with a good disposition. He seemed to be a responsible person, as he worked hard and was dedicated to his work.

The parents allowed their daughter and the charcoal burner to meet to see if they would make a good couple together. The meeting went well and the two hit it off.

After the meeting, the parents asked the daughter what she thought of the man.

The girl replied, "He certainly was a fine young man."

The parents became excited, thinking they had finally found a good match for her.

They asked, "What do you think about marrying him?"

She said, "I think he is really kind and has steady work, but I cannot marry him." The faces of the parents fell in disappointment. They thought if she would just say yes, their responsibilities as parents to settle their daughter would be fulfilled.

The parents asked, "If he is a good man with a stable business, why can't you marry him?"

She said, "As we were talking, we began discussing our work. You know that I clean houses and want my own house to be clean. I could not think of marrying him, because while I am taking great pains to make my house clean and spotless, he would be burning charcoal, and the dust and ashes would darken everything that I had cleaned. It just won't work!"

The same problem exists between our mind and our soul. This story describes what happened when the soul and the mind are married to each other within each human being. The mind is like the charcoal burner, trying to fill us with soot and grime, while the soul is the cleaner always trying to cleanse us. That tussle is always going on within us.

Imagine what kind of life the house-cleaning girl and the charcoal-burning man would have. She would clean and he would make soot. She would clean off the grime, and he would add more to it. Thus, their life would be a continuous struggle to get along with each other.

This continual struggle is going on within each of us daily. The soul is trying to be cleansed of all the soot created by the mind. At the same time, each time we clean off another portion of our thoughts, words, and deeds, the mind creates more filth.

What kind of grime does the mind create? The mind causes soot from the five thieves: anger, lust, greed, attachment, and ego. These drive our thoughts, words, and deeds. When we try to cleanse our mind through meditation, these thoughts distract us. We need to still our mind when we meditate, but we are hampered by thoughts of anger. We try to focus our attention within, but when we recollect what others at work or at home have said to us, we become angry. These angry thoughts rankle in our heads and we end up thinking about them instead of gazing at the inner Light in our meditation.

We try to meditate and we start thinking of all the things we want but do not have. Instead of meditating on the inner Light, we are thinking about how we can get what others have. Greed takes over and we lose focus on meditating.

When we try to meditate, we may also find ourselves thinking about all our attachments. We remember all the things we own or the people in our lives. When our thoughts are pulled by the people or possessions we love, we have trouble concentrating on our meditation.

We may start thinking about how wonderful we are. Instead of meditating we are thinking of how much better we are than other people. We start thinking we are more beautiful, more handsome, more intelligent, or stronger than others. We start admiring ourselves instead of gazing at the beautiful inner Light. Rather than admiring the Creator whose Light is shining within, we are admiring our own selves.

The soul wants to be cleansed of all these thoughts of the mind. It tries to meditate so that it can focus on the Light within, but the mind is strong. The soul needs help. How can we deal with this problem so we can stay in that state of purity when the mind is trying to defile us? We need a system whereby the mind can be stilled and unaffected by the grime from burning the coal. In this way, we can reach a state where we can enjoy the purity of our being. We can reach the state of purity of our soul, when we delve into spirituality. We can make "spiritually delve" as one of our goals in life. To spirituality delve means to delve into spirituality, or dive into spirituality. If we make diving into spirituality a priority in our life, it means we weed out anything that does not take us to that goal.

This is a path of positive mysticism, in which we lead a balanced life attending to our education, job or career, family, and helping others. Along with that, we devote maximum time to the spiritual side of our life. This means spending time in meditation, developing ethical values, and engaging in spiritual pursuits such as going to satsang and doing selfless service to help us grow spiritually. If we delve into our spiritual lives, we could weed out those extra things we do with our time that do not help us spiritually and focus on those that move us forward towards self-knowledge and God-realization.

The Master Cleaner helps us overcome the grime caused by the mind. On our own, we have a hard time stilling our mind. We need the strong help of the Master Power to help us achieve our goal.

How does the Master help us?

First, he connects us with the Naam or Word, the Light and Sound of God. When we meditate, we focus on the inner Light and Sound. Even while gazing, the mind wants to distract us with its thoughts. To remedy this, the Master teaches us the simran practice, the mental and silent repetition of the five Charged

Words given at initiation. Mental repetition of these Charged Words, carrying the spiritual radiation of the Master, uplifts our attention from the mind and body to focus at the third or single eye where we catch hold of the inner Light. The mind wants to think its thoughts of anger, lust, greed, attachment, and ego, but the repetition of the five Charged Words does not allow any thoughts to intervene. The simran practice keeps our mind engaged in these Words so no thoughts can work their way into our consciousness.

Along with the five Charged Words, the grace of the Master gives us a spiritual boost. His attention pulls our soul from awareness of the body, mind, and world to stay focused at the third or single eye.

The Master knows that the marriage of the soul and the mind is a challenge, just as the marriage between the charcoal burner and the house cleaner was doomed to be a challenge for their entire lives. Rather than leaving the mind and soul in a continual tussle, the Master comes to our rescue. He provides the needed help so that the house cleaner or our soul can make our house clean and organize the dust creation of the charcoal burner.

Our mind and our soul need a Master to help them learn to live productively together. Along with the five Charged Words and the grace, the Master also teaches us how to lead a life in which we help the mind recognize the importance of the soul. He shows us how to lead a life of nonviolence, truthfulness, purity, humility, and selfless service. This brings the mind under discipline. To help us track our thoughts, the Master gives us an introspection diary so we can record our status in these five positive virtues. In this way, we can keep our mind in check from anger, lust, greed, attachment, and ego.

The Master also teaches that selfless service empties us of the effects of the mind. When we serve without any material desire for monetary gain and fame, and without any ego, we keep the mind in check, letting the soul remain cleansed. The more time spent in selfless service, the more we help our soul.

Through meditation, selfless service, and doing the introspection diary, the soul can be kept clean. This creates a happy marriage between the mind and the soul. Our house is clean and spotless for God.

Let us spiritually delve so we weed out all the thoughts, words, and deeds that keep us from attaining the bliss of union of our soul with God.

Part 6

BE A
Spiritual Star

Part 6

BE A
Spiritual Star

THE MORNING ZEPHYR

Lo! Even the morning zephyr
has learned the ways of the Beloved,
Teasing the heart as it gently passes by!
– Sant Darshan Singh Ji Maharaj

God is love, the soul being of the same essence as God is love, and the way back to God is through love. Love is the cornerstone of our existence. This verse talks about the spiritual love between a disciple and the Master, the love between a spiritual disciple and God, and how through that love the Master helps the disciple be pulled quickly, strongly, and deeply back to God. In this way, we can experience our true self and be closer to God.

In this verse from a ghazal by Sant Darshan Singh Ji Maharaj, he takes a beautiful example of a zephyr, which is an early morning breeze. Generally, at night the breeze is still. In the morning, however, a small light breeze flows in, known as the easterly winds. In this verse, he describes a scene from olden times when people in warm climates mostly slept outside of their homes. In those days there were no air-conditioners, so most people slept outside as it was too warm to sleep indoors. When you sleep outside at night there is no wind blowing. In the morning, a gentle wind comes and touches your face and it feels good. Then, the wind stops. A while later, the wind blows again, strikes your face again, and you feel good again. Then, again it stops, pauses, and hits against your face one more time. It looks like it is teasing you. It comes, touches you a little bit, and then it is gone. Then, you want more of it. It comes back, touches you a little more, and then is gone again. That is what the analogy of the zephyr is. These easterly winds come and caress you, they stop, and they come and caress you more, and then stop. Sant Darshan Singh Ji takes this example of the zephyr and relates it to the love the Master Power has for disciples and how by its loving ways it creates a passion in us to know God and experience that Godly love.

Much of mystic poetry is spiritually romantic in nature. Sant Darshan Singh Ji, being a mystic poet, uses mystic symbolism to express the spiritual path. Just as the tavern image was used in a verse because that was a common experience to which people could relate to understand the relationship between the soul and God, so does this image of the zephyr provide a frame of reference to grasp another aspect of the mystic way. This set of images provides an opportunity to portray aspects of the Master-disciple relationship that are generally difficult to express. This verse answers the question: How does the Master Power enchant the disciple so he or she can be focused towards God?

Sant Darshan Singh Ji would say that love emanates from the heart of the Beloved. The Master Power wants our soul to be with God, so it creates a stirring in our heart and soul. That love from the Master Power comes to us first and we respond to that love.

In this verse, he describes how the Master Power starts to play with us. This play of the wind or zephyr is compared to the teasing of a beloved. Sometimes the worldly beloved may tease and then withdraw. Thus, the lover feels unsatisfied and starts to yearn and pine more and more for the beloved's attention. Why does the Master Power want to play with us? We receive some attention, but then it appears as if it stops. Then, we think, "Why did it stop? What did I do wrong? Maybe it was because I did not meditate or I am not doing my introspection diary." This helps us. We may think, "I was in the satsang and the Master looked at everyone else except me. Why? He looked there; he looked here; he patted this person; he patted that person; but, when he came to me, he did not even not look at me!" We start to think, "What did I do wrong?" and that starts us making an effort to improve ourselves. Thus, the Master Power is creating that spiritual passion in us. To express this, Sant Darshan Singh Ji uses the example of the zephyr, or easterly early morning wind. He describes this as another aspect of the spiritual path. If we are aware of it, then we will know when that happens that it is for our well-being. A true disciple knows that the Master Power loves everyone. The true disciples look at themselves. They say, "Okay, how can I improve now? These thoughts, many times, impel us to meditate more and introspect to become a better, more ethical person, so we can accelerate our progress.

Sant Darshan Singh Ji uses that example in this verse to clarify another aspect of spirituality. Spirituality is love, because God is nothing but love. The path of love unfolds in many different ways. When we read the writings of the great saints, we receive inklings into that love.

In the writings of mystics through the ages, we find references to the rapture experienced when we meet the Beloved on our inner journey. There is an anecdote from the life of a great woman saint of the East named Rabia Basri. Spring had arrived, and arrays of flowers bloomed everywhere. The air was fresh with a gentle breeze. Children played happily. Rabia, though, spent the day indoors in her meditation. One of Rabia's friends noticed that Rabia was indoors.

"O Rabia," she said, "It is so lovely out today. Why don't you come out and observe God's handiwork in nature?"

Rabia replied, "It would be better if you come in here with me, go within, and see the Creator for yourself. When I am indoors, I meditate and go into the regions Beyond and see the beautiful sights within. The love I experience within has no comparison to any beauty and love in the outer world. When I meditate, I behold God's glory within, which is so attractive I cannot even think of opening my eyes to see God's outer creation!"

As we go into the inner regions, the love of the Lord unfolds. As we go from the physical to the astral, we enter a region where our desires materialize. Every desire that we think about happens in the astral realm. As we rise from the astral to the causal realm, where the mind is the ruler, all our thoughts are implemented. It is only when we go beyond that to the supracausal realm and the spiritual realm of Sach Khand that we go beyond our mind and reach the region of pure spirit. During our spiritual journey, the layers of mind, matter, and illusion are peeled away. They fall off when we go within. If we just think that by being ethical alone we will reach our goals, that is not possible. Sant Kirpal Singh Ji clearly said, "An ethical life is a stepping-stone to spirituality." It is only the first step. Being good is important, but if we only inculcate the ethical virtues but do not meditate, we will not be able to rise above physical consciousness to reach God. Being good is good—we need that base. If we do not have that base we will not reach the goal, but we also have to take further steps of meditating to go within. Being ethical alone is not our only ultimate goal; that is just like a turn on a road leading up the mountain of our divine journey. There are further heights we need to reach.

One aspect of the spiritual path is divine love—the love that the Master Power and God have for each of us. Sant Darshan Singh Ji, in this verse, tells us of the intricacies of that divine love and how it manifests in our being. He explains there are many tools the Master Power has to fine tune us, and whatever is right for us plays out in our lives. There are many ways that a saint can draw us to God. They use whatever is the easiest and right one for us, so each of the disciples can experience the love of God.

How does the behavior of the zephyr relate to the Master or the Beloved? The analogy here is of the Master bestowing some grace and then withdrawing or holding it back. The disciple begins to pine for more. The Beloved may give us just enough spiritual energy to hold on, but then withdraws it. This may be in the form of a fleeting glance or a passing glance, leaving us yearning for deeper glances. It may be in the form of the Master appearing within in his radiant form for a moment, and then withdrawing, leaving us hungering for more. It can come in the form of glimpses of Light that come and go. The condition of the disciple is often one of a thirsting person. The more they drink, the more they want to drink. Thus, the disciple is never satiated. When the disciple wants more, it drives him or her to spend more time meditating to travel on the inner journey. The Master at times plays the role of giving and withholding, to create in us a more intense yearning that propels us faster on our spiritual travels.

The relationship between the Master and disciple is not a static one. It is one that is always changing, ever fresh and new. It is a relationship of trust. It is one in which the disciple reposes full faith in the Master to protect him or her and take care of his or her best interests. With this understanding, a disciple grasps the significance of the play of the zephyr. We have full confidence that the Master cares of us and is helping our soul reunite with God.

HIS BLESSINGS IN MEDITATION

O Darshan, what can be said about
his blessings in meditation?
I just close my eyes and the radiant form
of the Beloved comes.
– Sant Darshan Singh Ji Maharaj

In this verse, Sant Darshan Singh Ji Maharaj explores meditation. This verse talks about the grace of the Master and how we need to put in an effort and not worry about the results. If we do so, results will come. All disciples want to be able to reach the radiant form of the Master to guide us, but we may not have reached it yet. We may be seeing inner Lights of any color, or seeing the inner sky, the stars, the inner moon, or the inner sun. These are all reflections of the divine Light. However, we need to go beyond these to reach the radiant form of the Master to be able to transcend into higher spiritual regions. That journey is timeless—we can reach that goal in months or years, or we can reach it in a second. For example, once someone asked Hazur Baba Sawan Singh Ji Maharaj how long it takes to get to Sach Khand. He closed his eyes and opened them again, and said, "I have just been there and came back." Therefore, it is not a question of time to get there; it is a question of attention. Sant Darshan Singh Ji says in this verse, "O Darshan, what can we say about his blessings in meditation?" This verse expresses that he reached there by closing his eyes and the radiant form of the Master appeared. All of us can reach that goal.

Along with regular meditation, one of the steps to reach God is to lead an ethical life. For that, we have been given an introspection diary, a tool by which we can weed out our shortcomings. When we fill it out daily at the end of the day, and do it truthfully, we know what our shortcomings are. Sant Kirpal Singh Ji used to say, "Work on one area of the diary at a time. Take one of the columns of the diary and try to perfect ourselves in that column. As we perfect ourselves in that column, we can select another column on which to work, and then the next one, the next one, and the next one." Slowly, we remove our shortcomings. As we do that, we develop an ethical base from which we can go on our spiritual journey. That ethical foundation is a stepping-stone necessary to spring into the regions Beyond.

At the same time that we are developing that ethical base, we need to find time daily for our meditation. The Master recommends that we meditate for ten percent of our daily time, which out of twenty-four hours comes to two and a half hours. Our task is to devote ourselves to meeting the Beloved within. Sant Kirpal Singh Ji said that until we reach that stage we are on probation. We are at the kindergarten level. We need to move on to the higher grades. A teacher may promote a student out of grace, but wants the student to put in an effort. The teacher has the power to move a student up to the next grade out of mercy and compassion, but if a student has not learned lessons at a lower grade and has not advanced, then that student may struggle at a higher grade. Thus, the teacher works with the student to help put in an effort until the student is ready to move up. It is a combination of effort and grace. Similarly, the Master has the power to take all souls back Home, but does not do so until we are ready. Readiness means that we need to perfect the method of meditation and have the needed purity to enter the pure realms Beyond.

For example, the inner realms are subtle. In the astral realm, every thought we have can manifest itself as reality. If we enter inner realms with anger and hatred, the power of those thoughts can do untold harm. The causal realm is one in which the mind is the ruler. Whatever the mind brings forth can become reality. You can imagine the havoc that can be played if an uncontrolled mind brings forth violence and destruction. As we go higher, we find purely spiritual realms where the mind has no influence. There are purely spiritual realms of love, nonviolence, truth, and compassion. Not even a particle of dust of hatred, violence, falsehood, and cruelty can enter such a realm. We cannot reach those realms until we have attained that level of purity. As one can see, there is much work we need to do to enter into the higher regions.

The journey through the spiritual realms requires focused concentration. If our meditations are not perfected, and we are still distracted by every passing thought, how can we keep our attention long enough to enjoy the Beyond? When we start to rise within, suddenly, a thought can pull us back down. Even the thought that, "Oh, I am rising above the body!" is a thought and will drag our attention back down into the body. Thus, we will not advance far within if we are still under the sway of mind and our thoughts, for those will distract us from the inner sights and sounds. Perfecting our meditation means that we sit with our body and mind still without any thoughts to distract us. How many can do that even for five minutes? The Master exhorts us to do our meditative practices. The more time we spend in accurate meditation, the more time we perfect our concentration so we can stay steadfast on the Light and Sound, the radiant form of the Master, and the inner vistas. The Master may, out of grace, suddenly pull us up, but we do not yet have the perfection of concentration to even stay there. Thus, Master exhorts us to do our practices so he can show us beautiful realms within and take us back to God.

Every teacher wants all the students to pass. No teacher wants any student to fail, to not do the homework, or to miss class. Similarly, a Master wants all disciples to achieve what he has attained. He tries every possible means to help us succeed, but he cannot force us to do our homework and our studies. He cannot force us to attend satsang, introspect to weed out our shortcomings, do selfless service, or meditate. He can only point the way. It is up to us to be committed to the practice to excel.

For success on the spiritual path, we need to perform our meditative practices and lead an ethical life. It is difficult to stick to our goals, in the face of challenges trying to sidetrack us. At every second, setbacks try to waylay us from our journey. We are distracted by numerous temptations and attractions that keep us from meditating and living ethically. Our job is to keep trying, no matter what obstacles come in our way.

In this connection, there is a story of a king who lived many years ago. He tried to take over other kingdoms and conquer the world. He built a strong army who conquered one kingdom after another. After winning many battles, the king encountered something he never anticipated; he went into battle and lost. His army of soldiers were about to become prisoners of war or killed. The soldiers who survived fled to save their lives. The king, with no one left to protect him, also fled alone into the wilderness to save his own life.

The king hid out, traveling only by night so no one would see him. He knew the conquering army was looking for him, so he kept running and hiding. He was not used to taking care of himself and having no one to wait on him. He had to scavenger for his own food and find places to sleep at night in the wilderness where no one could find him.

One day, as he rested under a tree, he began to feel sorry for himself. He knew that he could not make himself seen as the other army would capture or kill him. Seeing no way out of his predicament, he began to lose hope. He had been wandering for twenty days, with no sign of making it through this crisis. The king thought that he might as well be caught as trying to survive alone in the jungle had become so difficult.

As he rested under the tree, feeling like he should give up, he noticed a small insect climbing the tree trunk. Looking closer, he saw it was a tiny ant. The ant carried a grain of wheat almost as big as itself. The insect struggled to carry the grain up the tree. Then, the king noticed there was a hole in the tree where pieces of grain were stored. He realized the ant carried these large pieces of grain up the tree to store in the hole.

The king watched with interest as the ant tried to make it up the tree to deposit the grain in the hole. He noticed that the ant had stored many grains in the hole in preparation for winter.

When the ant had reached a short distance from the hole, it fell down from the tree, with the grain falling with it.

The king marveled at the ant's bravery in carrying a load as large as its own body.

Even after falling, the ant retrieved the grain and carried it up the tree again. It reached a certain distance and again toppled to the ground.

Not giving up, the ant picked up the grain and started up the tree. Each time it hit a rough spot on the tree, it plunged back down.

Yet, the ant still did not give up. It kept trying time and time again to carry the grain up the tree to put into the hole where he was saving the food.

The king watched for hours as the ant continued to try again and again and again. The ant tried to climb with the grain five times, ten times, fifteen times, and at the twentieth time, it fell again. Yet, every time it fell, it did not give up. It would try to find a slightly different path each time, thinking it might work.

Finally, on its twenty-first try, the ant climbed again, carefully crawling through the rough patch, until finally scurrying into the hole, put the piece of grain there.

The king felt relieved and happy for the ant, and cried out, "Great job!" to the ant.

The king thought about what he had seen and said to himself, "Why am I feeling so hopeless? The ant has taught me a great lesson today. If the ant can fall twenty times, I should try to save myself. No matter how bad things look, I should try again and again until I succeed." Seeing the example of the ant kept him going until he was able to escape, making it back to his kingdom.

We also need to put in an effort when it comes to meditation. The lesson of the ant can serve to motivate us when we feel as if in a slump. On the spiritual path, we need to meditate each day for a minimum of two and a half hours to reach the goal of reunion of our soul with God in this lifetime. Our difficulty is that we give up too easily. We may meditate far less than the required time and wonder why we have not yet reunited with God. We may sit for five minutes with eyes closed and then say, "We haven't seen anything yet, so let's stop meditating." We may sit for the required time, but find that our mind is not meditating; instead, it is thinking of this thing or that. Then, we think we have put in so many hours, but are still not in our eternal Home yet.

The secret to meditation is to be steady and accurate. Both are required for success.

When we are not making headway, we may feel like giving up, just as the king wanted to pack it all in and give up. It was by seeing the numerous attempts and failures of the ant, until finally the ant reached its goal, that kept the king going.

We should steadily keep going. Each time we fall, we think it is the end. We need to pick ourselves up, brush ourselves off, and start all over again. We never know when the right time will come when we will be rewarded with success.

We need to remember that the fruits of our efforts are in God's hands. Our job is to do our duty, to meditate regularly and accurately. If we do so, God will present us with the experiences at the right time. If we do not sit to meditate, how can we receive anything? We need to be present and available by sitting in meditation for God. God may be ready to give us everything today, but we are not even sitting in meditation to receive.

The goal of the mystic experience is to find the divine Beloved within. God is the eternal Beloved. Since we cannot see spirit,

God works through a Master Power to manifest and be known. Thus, in every age, the Power of God radiates through the form of selected human poles who can connect seekers back to God. God has worked through numerous forms in the past and will continue to work through numerous forms in the future. God's message has been conveyed to humanity through the ages. They serve as guides to bring souls back to God. It is a great blessing to have inner guidance of one who knows the roadway Home.

Sant Darshan Singh Ji in this verse refers to meeting the inner form of the guide in meditation. The inner radiant form of the Master is an experience that cannot be described adequately in words. It is not merely something that we see; it is a deep experience of the soul that has transformative and uplifting powers. The radiant form has attractive energy that pulls soul from the chains of the world to let it soar freely into the spiritual regions Beyond. We are engrossed in the shackles of mind, matter, and illusion. On our own, we cannot free ourselves from the pull of the world. The magnetic power of the radiant form uplifts our soul from its entanglement to let us experience the blissful realms within.

The experience of meeting the radiant form of the Master is a profound experience of love. God's love penetrates every pore of our being. Imagine a loving moment with a worldly beloved. That is but a small taste of tremendous love we experience when we meet the radiant form within. It is like that worldly love but multiplied a thousandfold. It is as if one loving experience is going on a thousand times simultaneously through every pore of us. It is so intense and intoxicating that many people when they first taste of this love cry out in rapture. We have seen people who have left their body to soar within experience so much love and intensity that they automatically let out cries of joy.

The goal of the spiritual path lies in having this rendezvous within with the Beloved. All our meditations, efforts in stilling the mind, in becoming a better person through keeping the introspection diary and living up to ethical values crystallizes in the inner meeting with Beloved. Once we meet the radiant form, we can begin the journey through spiritual regions to God. Then, we realize what divine love is. We become a vessel through which the love of God can flow to all humanity and creation. That is the stage at which we truly love all.

We need to forge ahead, day by day, without worrying about the results. Our job is to meditate; it is God's job to give. Let us not give up if we have a bad day. We need to keep going.

The same principal holds true when we are doing our diary. We may mark our daily introspection diary each evening and think that if the numbers do not improve we should give up. We should not take a defeatist attitude, but rather be like the ant. We should make an attempt to reduce our failures each day, even by one. We should not set too high a goal for ourselves that will frustrate us if we fail. We should each day attempt to improve in a category. We can concentrate on one category and then try to reach zero mistakes. Then, we can take another category and work on that. Even if we see our numbers in a category go up, we should not give up. It may be that the failures are not increasing, but our discerning eye that recognizes the failures is become more accurate. We may have overlooked some subtle failures before and are becoming more cognizant of them. We still need to plunge ahead until we ultimately reach our goal of zero failures in each category. It is attainable. We need to keep going and not give up.

Let us take the lesson of the ant in all areas of our life. Whether it is meditation, ethical living, or our daily responsibilities and mundane goals in life, we should stay positive, forge ahead, and keep trying no matter what.

If we find that we are currently still at the kindergarten level, what should we do? The lesson plans are clear. We need to put in at least two and a half hours daily accurate meditation and keep the introspection diary to develop ethical virtues. Those are the homework assignments. If we would do these faithfully, we would find the radiant form of the Master waiting within. If we have not reached there yet, let us analyze how accurately our homework has been done and how accurate our meditations have been. We can see which areas of the diary still need to be perfected. Then we can take action to start from today to reach the goal.

We may think we are sitting for meditation, but are we spending time thinking of the past or the future? Are we lost in fears and worries? All these are impediments to concentration. We need to put our fears and worries aside during the time we spend in meditation. We can either write them down before we meditate and say to ourselves that we will deal with them after meditation, or just put them in an imaginary drawer and close it until the meditation period is over. It is useless to sit for meditation and spend the whole time thinking. It is better to spend five minutes in accurate concentrated meditation than to spend two hours in thinking of the past and future, because then we are not really meditating at all. If we cannot put in the full two and a half hours in one sitting, or two sittings of one and a quarter hour each, then we can break up the two and a half hours. We can sit three times for fifty minutes, or four times for about thirty-eight minutes, or five times at a half hour a piece, when we have days or schedules where we cannot put in one or two full sittings. The two and a half hours a day is a minimum. The more time we can do than that, the better. Let us start from today onward with a new resolution to concentrate on accuracy and go on increasing the time that we can meditate correctly.

If we want to see the radiant form of the Beloved within, then the instructions are clear. We need to be devoted to meditation and be committed to leading the kind of life that makes us fit to enter God's kingdom. In this way, we will attract God's grace so God can bring us back to our Eternal Home.

Sant Rajinder Singh Ji Maharaj

ABOUT THE AUTHOR
SANT RAJINDER SINGH JI MAHARAJ

Sant Rajinder Singh Ji Maharaj is an internationally-recognized spiritual Master of meditation on the inner Light and Sound, president of the Human Unity Conference, and head of Science of Spirituality, a non-profit, non-denominational organization that provides a forum for people to learn meditation, experience personal transformation, and bring about inner and outer peace and human unity.

He has presented his powerful, yet simple meditation on the inner Light and Sound to millions of people throughout the world through seminars, meditation retreats, television and radio shows and Internet broadcasts, magazines, and books.

His method of achieving inner and outer peace through meditation has been recognized by civic and spiritual leaders. He convened the 16th International Human Unity Conference in Delhi, India; was president of the 7th World Religions Conference; was a major presenter at the Parliament of the World Religions held in Chicago in 1993 and the World Conference on Religion and Peace held in Rome and Riva del Garde, Italy, in 1994. He hosts annual international conferences on Human Integration and Global Mysticism. At the 50th Anniversary of the United Nations celebration held at the Cathedral of St. John the Divine, Sant Rajinder Singh Ji opened the program by putting thousands of people into meditation. He has received numerous awards, tributes, and honorary welcomes from civic heads around the world.

He is a best-selling author whose many books include, *Spark of the Divine, Inner and Outer Peace through Meditation, Empowering Your Soul through Meditation, Meditation as Medication for the Soul, Silken Thread of the Divine, Spiritual*

Pearls for Enlightened Living, Spiritual Thirst, Visions of Spiritual Unity and Peace, Ecology of the Soul, Education for a Peaceful World, and many books in Hindi, including *Spirituality in Modern Times* and *True Happiness*. His publications have been translated into fifty languages. He also has many CDs, DVDs, and hundreds of articles published in magazines, newspapers, and journals throughout the world. He has appeared on television, radio, and Internet broadcasts worldwide. Sant Rajinder Singh Ji holds meditation seminars and gives public lectures throughout North America, South America, Europe, Africa, Asia, Australia, and Oceania.

He can be contacted at Kirpal Ashram, Sant Kirpal Singh Marg, Vijay Nagar, Delhi, India 110009; Tel: 91-11-27117100; or FAX: 91-11-7214040; or at the Science of Spirituality Center, 4 S. 175 Naperville Rd., Naperville, IL 60563; Tele: (630) 955-1200; or FAX: (630) 955-1205. Or visit www.sos.org.